Early
Mathematical
Experiences

Addison-Wesley Publishers Limited
London · Reading, Massachusetts · Menlo Park, California · Don Mills, Ontario · Amsterdam ·
Singapore · Sydney · Tokyo

Contents

Longman Group UK Limited
Longman House, Burnt Mill, Harlow, Essex CM20 2JE,
England and Associated Companies throughout the world.
© Third edition SCDC Publications 1990
First edition © Schools Council Publications 1978
Second edition © Schools Council Publications 1982
The first and second editions were published for the
Schools Council by Addison – Wesley Publishers Limited.
Produced by Longman Singapore Publishers Pte Ltd
Printed in Singapore

ISBN 0 582 05819 8

The EME project was established by the
Schools Council in 1974 at Chelsea College,
University of London, where it ran until 1979.

Directors
Geoffrey Matthews
Julia Matthews

Team members
Audrey Nicole
Jill Hancock
Margaret Adams
Yvonne Wardrop
Bob Perry
Isobel Provan—Secretary

Acknowledgement
Much of the material used in EME came direct from
the classroom. Considerations of space prevent
individual acknowledgements, but the directors of
the project take this opportunity of expressing their
warmest thanks for all the help which they have
received.

Illustrated by Nina Sowter
Photographs by John Birdsall

Part 1
Introducing EME

Introduction

Early Mathematical Experiences (EME) was a three year project funded by the Schools Council. This book is a re-organised and up-dated version of the booklets which this project produced.

There are many ways of approaching the teaching of mathematics to young children and indeed a number of Local Education Authorities have produced valuable guidelines. This book provides a basis which will slot into any scheme and provide support in the form of practical suggestions and starting points.

History of EME

The original Nuffield Mathematics Project (age range 5–13 identified the need to help very young children develop mathematical concepts and overcome the handicap of those who start formal education without relevant experiences, activities and conversation. A White Paper with proposals for the expansion of education of the very young child had suggested that a project designed to meet this need would be timely, and the work done by Miss Marianne Parry and Miss Hilda Archer in the Schools Council's Pre-School Education Project (1969–71) further underlined the needs of the very young child.

Accordingly the Schools Council funded not only the Communication Skills in Early Childhood Project, directed by Dr Tough, but also this project concerned with early mathematical experiences.

Aims

The general aim of the project was to study relevant experiences leading to mathematical ideas for young children and to help their teachers with suggestions on how to foster these experiences. More specifically, the aims were:

1 To identify and classify relevant experiences leading to mathematical ideas by observing young children in the classroom and relating their work to the theoretical development of early mathematical concepts.

2 To produce guidance for teachers to help them to stimulate the development of mathematical concepts in young children.

Working groups

When the project started, 24 pilot groups and 43 associate groups were set up. To carry out the first aim outlined above, it was necessary to spend some time building up a collection of experiences and conversations, as little research was available on "early mathematics". This was entirely an advantage, as the teachers in the working groups could not help feeling directly involved and their efforts were vital to the success of the project.

What is meant by early mathematical experiences?

Children begin to absorb mathematical ideas from a very early age and as their use and understanding of language progresses, so they are able to convey these ideas to other children and people around them. Very young children often complain bitterly, for example, if given a different sort of cake from that offered to the rest of the family, or if not given their own special cup. They have already begun to appreciate differences and are on their way to sorting, if only into "what I like" and "don't like"!

The same learning process goes on as they explore the whole gamut of toys, books, music and physical activity, gaining experience in the way materials may be manipulated. This gradual collecting and storing up of information leads children towards acquiring concepts. "Concept" is used here to describe an idea which is abstracted from a variety of related and repeated experiences.

Mathematics for very young children is an incidental and integral part of their general activity and they need a variety of experiences from which they may generalise later. At this stage their play may be free and experience apparently random, but it is in this range of experience that they encounter ideas (such as, "inside", "next to", "taller than", "heavier than") in a variety of contexts, and from which they gradually acquire concepts.

Through their play, children encounter many new ideas, and consolidate others. Some of these ideas (or concepts) are essential for the later understanding of mathematics. A simple example of a concept is that of *matching*. For instance, a child may give a plate to each doll at a tea-party. They have been *matched* so that there is the same number of dolls as plates. To each doll there corresponds a plate. (This is why matching is sometimes called one-to-one correspondence.)

Without this concept, the business of counting becomes meaningless. When it is grasped, however, saying the numbers one, two, three, four, five, etc. can be synchronised with objects and counting becomes reliable.

When children first come to school, an obvious priority is to help each child to feel secure and to provide a great variety of activities, trying to cater for the needs of each individual. As children become used to school, they will be led to discover new ways of experimenting with familiar materials. Then, with talking to adults about things that they notice, and through making choices, each child begins to progress in his thinking and reasoning.

After watching a group of children building and demolishing towers of blocks day after day (a very satisfying experience in emotional and sensory terms for the child), a teacher may seek to extend their experience in some way. If she places the basket of blocks in a corner already occupied by a small table and chair, some child may use the blocks in such a way as to suggest the outline of a house. The opportunity may then be ripe for the adult to suggest refinements such as a doorway (Can I come inside as well?). As the play develops, there may be discussion about the height of the roof, separate rooms for sleeping and eating, a garage or a garden with a boundary fence. However, the teacher must be careful not to force her ideas on a child who is engaged in acquiring experiences in his own way at his own speed. Such activities are leading towards a conception of space and eventually geometrical ideas such as volume, size and perspective.

Opinions vary deeply on the amount of adult guidance which should be given to young children. Clearly it is absurd to interrupt a child in the process of creation, with a mathematical question, but it is equally unhelpful to provide a proliferation of activities and then stand back, leaving children to experiment in a way that does little to help their natural stages of development. There must be a degree of structure in the adult's mind and the middle-way philosophy adopted by EME is to suggest that careful thought be given to the mathematics that is *inherent* in any activity or material that children are offered. Then, if a child shows a particular interest in the mathematical side or asks questions, he can be guided towards this idea and helped to explore the language that goes with it. For example, a child may play at the sand and water trays for many days, experimenting with plastic pots of varying sizes, with and without holes pierced in them, before he is introduced to words like, "full", "empty", "fast", "faster", "slow", "slowly", etc.

Whatever views may be held about the amount of adult intervention that is ideal, there is no doubt that there is progression in children's thinking and doing during the early years and their activities must be related to their current capabilities.

Concepts and Vocabulary

Concepts and progression

The years from three to six are vital ones; horizons widen daily and physical and intellectual changes are most marked. Not surprisingly, great strides are made during this period towards the acquisition of concepts including, of course, mathematical ones. However, as all children are not only different but develop at different rates, it would be fruitless to attempt to pinpoint the various stages of progression and relate them to age. There is, indeed, a good case for young children to be encouraged generally to find their own level within the environment provided, as is the policy and practice of many excellent teachers. When playing with and discussing materials in the classroom, the children will certainly have some kind of experience, but all the same the depth of the experience and the progression will depend very largely upon a meaningful encounter with an understanding adult. Without this careful guidance, children could play their way through this stage of education with very little progress. The onus is, therefore, on the teacher, and the main purpose of EME is to show possibilities for children's experiences designed to foster progress.

The policy adopted in EME is, therefore, to give outlines of progression within each topic. It is left to the teacher, knowing her children's strengths and weaknesses, to determine when and, indeed, *if* to intervene.

The mathematical concepts concerned can be listed quite briefly but their importance cannot be over-emphasised. Their acquisition comes only from a wide variety of experiences.

Much trouble is stored up if children are hurried over the early stages and asked to perform tasks without understanding. Matching has already been mentioned, but to give a further example: a child is "counting" bricks; to do this with understanding he must be able to match each brick in turn with the successive numbers, 1, 2, 3 . . . . The mere ability to chant numbers rapidly is not enough, in fact the skill of counting is dependent on the *idea* of matching (sometimes called one-to-one correspondence or pairing).

This has brought in one of the basic concepts, namely matching. The following is a list of such major concepts that are relevant at EME level.

1	Matching	4	Ordering
2	Sorting	5	Recognition of shapes
3	Comparisons	6	Invariances

Sorting is fundamental, not only to mathematics but almost any other activity. At this level sorting will be of the type like/dislike, red/not red, float/sink, blue eyes/not blue eyes. (See also page 8 below).

Comparisons include relationships such as "is taller than", "is heavier than", "is longer than", "has more than". The statement "this house is large" does not necessarily convey a lot (how large is large?), but "this house is larger than that one" is precise and can be verified. Each comparison can be put in two ways, for example if "Jack has more sweets than Jill", then "Jill has fewer sweets than Jack". Such pairs of statements should be encouraged.

Ordering comes in numbers, spatial relationships and measurement. The obvious example of ordering is the sequence 1st, 2nd, 3rd ... but before this has meaning, children have many experiences: for example, of ordering themselves according to height, weight, etc, or making simple measurements with hand-spans ("John's shadow is 8 hand-spans, then comes Jill with 7 and Tom with just over 6.").

Recognition of shapes involves familiarity with simple solids, (cubes, spheres, etc.) and two-dimensional figures such as squares and triangles. The *recognition* of a triangle, for example, implies that the child will still recognise it as a triangle when it is turned upside-down.

Invariances. These are sometimes called "conservations". For example to understand the invariance of length a child has to appreciate that a stick will remain the same length even if moved round. Invariance of number means that if there are 5 bricks on a table, there will still be 5 (and no need to recount) if they are simply shuffled round. Other invariances include weight (liquids and solids), volume and area. None of these invariances will be fully understood at this level, but they are included here as it is important to provide early experiences, (e.g. with sand, water, balances) through which understanding will eventually come.

A brief discussion as to how these concepts develop beyond EME and relate to mathematical skills is given in the section *Where's all this leading to?*.

Children's vocabulary

Mathematics should arise from the children's activities and alongside the development of their vocabulary. Such words as "above", "below", "next to", "under", "over" etc. are mathematical relationships which crop up naturally in the course of events. Many examples are given in the chapters which follow.

Adult vocabulary

Teachers may well come across some mathematical terms with which they may not be familiar. Although these will not be used with the children, they may help the teacher to clarify ideas. Some of these terms have already been described under "basic concepts". Those most frequently found in the topic chapters are given below together with references to the chapters where relevant activities and experiences may be found. The list is as follows:

> *Matching, Ordering, Invariances, Relations, Sorting, Transitivity, Cardinal number of a set, Geometry.*

Matching

References in topic chapters
Home Corner: pp. 55, 56, 58, 62
Towards Number: pp. 103, 104
Outdoor Activities: pp. 122, 123, 125
Water: p. 78
Raw Materials: p. 93
Rhymes and Stories: p. 161

Ordering

Relations (relationships)

Richard (3.6): "Ian's teddy is smaller than Jason's."

Mathematics is the study of relations. What, exactly, is a relation? Some examples may help in the explanation of this difficult idea.

Examples
We talk about *family relations*—brothers, sisters, mum, dad, etc. These are concerned with the ways in which people can be "connected".

Number relations are statements which show how two or more numbers are "connected".

2 and 3 are "connected" by the relation "is less than", since 2 is less than 3.
2, 3 and 5 are "connected" by the operation "addition" and the relation "equals" since 2 + 3 = 5.

Invariances

For further exploration of this difficult idea, see *Mathematics—the First Three Years*, Nuffield Mathematics Project and C.E.D.O., Chambers and Murray, 1970.

Spatial relationships
Ginette (4.5) on the seesaw: "I am up in the air, and David is down on the ground ... Now I am down and David is up."

Spatial relations "connect" sub-sets of space. "Higher than" is a spatial relation which is met quite often by very young children when playing on climbing apparatus. "Has more sides than" is a relation used to discuss shapes.

Sorting

Isobel (3.2): "What's that doing in here? Nothing same as that in here—take it out!" Isobel has found a duck which was not part of the sets of sorting animals and birds—it was a pastry cutter.

Sorting has already been mentioned as a basic concept. Most children have done a lot of sorting long before they ever come to school. For example, children decide that some toys are soft and cuddly or that others roll or are bouncy.

When objects are sorted, they are put into *sets*. *A set is a collection of things*. The "things" in the set are called *elements*. These elements need not have anything in common except that they belong to the set.

For example:

A set of three pigs

The set of letters in the word Paul:

[P, a, u, l] or, for example, [a, P, l, u]

The set containing a bucket, a tin and a spoon:

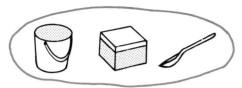

When children sort a set of objects into two or more smaller sets we say that they are *partitioning* the first set into *sub-sets*.

For example: The set

could be partitioned into the two sub-sets

A set is said to be *included* in another set if *every* element of the first set is an element of the second set. For example:

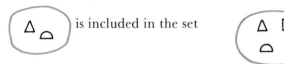

The *union of the two sets* is the set containing all the elements which are in either set or in both.
For example:

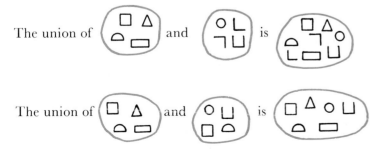

The intersection of two sets is the set containing the elements which are in *both* sets.

For example:

the *empty set*—the set containing no elements.

References in topic chapters

Water: pp. 78, 81, 83
Raw Materials: p. 89
Home Corner: pp. 57, 58
Towards Number: pp. 101, 102
Apparatus, Toys and Games: pp. 114, 115
Outdoor Activities: p. 124
The Environment: pp. 133, 137
The Passage of Time: p. 148

Transitivity

This idea becomes important when a child is dealing with more than two sets (or numbers). Suppose there are three sets, A, B and C, and suppose also that we know (by matching) A has as many elements as B and B has as many elements as C. Then, we should be able to see that A has as many elements as C. When a child can consistently argue this (without a third matching of elements from A and C), we say that he has developed the *concept of transitivity*. Transitivity will become important later with other relations, in particular the inclusion (inequality) relation. Thus, from the statements $3 < 4$ and $4 < 7$, children should eventually be able to argue that $3 < 7$.

There are no references to transitivity in EME, as this stage of reasoning is not usually reached until after the age of five. *Checking Up, 1* (Nuffield Mathematics Project, *Checking Up, 1*, (p.34), W & R Chambers and J. Murray, 1970) give details of a summary check-up for one-to-one correspondence and transitivity. One teacher tried this with a group of rising fives and only one child came near to showing understanding. This is a transcript of their conversation, dealing first with one-to-one correspondence.

Example

Daniel (4.8) was considered to have a well-developed sense of number, so that I was surprised when he thought there were more bricks than counters when I spread out the bricks.

Teacher: Are they still the same? Are there as many bricks as there are counters?
Daniel: No, 'cos there's more bricks.
Teacher: Are you sure? Shall we match them together again?
Daniel: Then it's the same.
Teacher: Is it the same if we do that—if we spread them out. Is that different?
Daniel: No, different.
Teacher: What? Are there more bricks now, or less?
Daniel: No, they are the same only they are spread out.
Teacher: Now see if you can put as many toys as there are bricks, for me, will you?

He matches toys to bricks.

Teacher: Now are they the same? The same toys as there are bricks?
Daniel: Yes.
Teacher: I'm going to take the bricks away and pile them up there. Now tell me, have we got the same number of counters as we've got toys?

Daniel (after some thought): Yes, but they are all spreaded out.
Teacher: How can you be sure?
Daniel: I used my brains, I used my brains to find out. You are meant to use them. I put the counters, bricks and toys into bundles.
Teacher: Is any bundle bigger than another bundle?
Daniel: That's the biggest bundle.
Teacher: Has it got the most things in?
Daniel: No, they are all the same things.

Daniel certainly understood the one-to-one correspondence, but had to search for words to explain himself. Again I found that I was using "more", "most" and "the same as" to try to help him explain, but he was able to internalise these words and use his own words to convey his thoughts.

Cardinal number of a set

Shafgar (4.1): "I done another one. Two paintings. I'll take these two paintings home."
The cardinal number of a set is simply the number of elements in the set.

For example:
The cardinal number of [*, *, *] is 3.
The cardinal number of [*, □, △, 0] is 4.

References in topic chapters

Geometry

Topology

Jason (4.8): "We've made a bridge. The cars go over the bridge and the boats go under."

Topology is the study of properties of geometric figures that remain unchanged under distortion. Such properties include the order of points, between-ness, closedness of curves, next to, ... but do not include any properties which depend on measurement (such as straightness of lines, angle sizes).

References in topic chapters

Water: p. 79
Space and Shape: p. 36
Outdoor Activities: pp. 125, 127

Tesselation

Pierce (4.3): "The rectangles and squares are best to hide the paper."

A *tesselation* is a way of covering a surface by repeating a certain figure—that is, a tiling pattern made by repeating a single shape. For example:

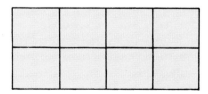

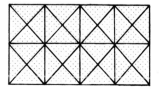

References in topic chapters

Space and Shape: p. 41
Comparisons: pp. 48, 49
Home Corner: p. 57

Translation

Shelley (4.9) making hand-prints

Translation is the single movement of an object without turning it.

Rotation

Matthew (4.7) holding up a triangular piece of paper by one vertex

"It's a triangle isn't it, but it is upside down."

Rotation is the moving of an object through an angle.

Reflection

Samina (4.8):
"Oh! Look, it fits!"

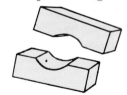

Reflection is the replacing of an object by its "image" as if it had been reflected in a mirror.

References in topic chapters

Water: p. 81
Space and Shape: pp. 42, 43
Home Corner: pp. 58, 62

Into action

Organization of the book

It must be stated, right at the beginning, that EME is *not* meant to be a scheme of work to be followed faithfully from cover to cover and in a particular order. It has been written to explain and demonstrate as many as possible of the mathematical ideas that young children need to absorb before starting maths in the more formal sense. On the other hand, it is of little use to read it like a novel and feel one has "done" EME. A quick glance through could certainly give a general view of the possibilities, but it is more a matter of attitude, of being continuously aware, so that bringing in a mathematical slant to everyday activities becomes second nature.

It should be remembered, however, that acquisition of mathematical concepts is only one part, although a major one, of a child's overall development. The sensitive teacher, while planning some activities with a definite bias towards maths, will be careful not to spoil imaginative and creative play by intruding at the wrong time, or trying to coerce children who are not yet ready into mathematical games.

Eight of the themes in the book (*Water, Home Corner, Outdoor Activities, Raw Materials, The Family, The Environment, Apparatus, Toys and Games* and *Rhymes and Stories*) deal with everyday activities, pointing out the mathematical ideas that arise in the normal day's routine. Thus, when planning a Home Corner, for example, it would be worth reading *Home Corner*, where the mathematical ideas which children could be encouraged to explore when certain equipment is provided, e.g. sets of cutlery and dolls of various sizes, are set out. At other times, a "dip" into *Outdoor Activities*, for example, can act as a reminder or a challenge to try an old activity in a new way.

The remaining four themes (*Space and Shape, Comparisons, Towards Number, The Passage of Time*) are presented as suggestions of activities leading towards specific mathematical concepts.

Each topic chapter concentrates on the acquisition of appropriate mathematical vocabulary. Young children need to be "doing and thinking", and adults who provide stimulating and challenging conversation help them to put these thoughts into words. There is a great skill in guiding conversations and asking questions which extend children's ideas. A little feigned ignorance (I wonder what will happen if I do that?) *can* work wonders, whereas a straightforward question with a yes or no answer may lead the child to abandon his play and move to an activity that is less likely to be interrupted.

"Do it yourself" is a good way of using the materials. Some of the pilot groups started with a topic, for instance, *Water*, and went through the sequence:

1 Observe the children in action.

2 Jot down short anecdotes, even on the back of an envelope.

3 Gradually note rather longer sequences: what led up to a particular incident? How was it followed up?

4 Only then look at the EME writing and compare notes.

An adult who is strong-minded enough to do this will profit far more than going straight for other people's experiences! But it is difficult to think things out alone, and it is strongly hoped that further study groups will be set up in teachers' centres to criticise, use, amend and extend the project's ideas. Courses for teachers, assistants, play-group leaders and parents can also help people not to feel isolated. Schools can help parents by holding brief meetings to familiarise them with the EME materials, so that some of the ideas can be extended into the home.

But having said all this, it is hoped that the writing has been sufficiently clear for everybody to get something from it, even if they have no-one with whom to discuss the ideas. Just being aware of the mathematical possibilities that arise and putting in the little unobtrusive questions at the end of an activity may make all the difference to the child's development, assurance and happiness.

Evaluation

"To study relevant experiences leading to mathematical ideas for young children and to help their teachers with suggestions on how to encourage these" was the original aim of the project. For evaluation, this original aim must be examined and an assessment made on how far this has been achieved.

To fulfil the aim of the EME project, many teachers pooled their experiences and ideas, helping in the collection and revision of materials for the book. Their suggestions and experiences were co-ordinated by a small project team who also spent time observing teachers and their assistants at work with young children. It was found that there were many different methods of presenting activities and learning situations to the children, but these could be grouped loosely into four main categories:

1 Children playing freely with as many activities and materials as possible, without adult intervention.

2 Children playing with materials which had been deliberately provided by teachers to encourage the acquisition of certain concepts, but still without adult intervention.

3 Children playing with materials of their own choice with the active participation of an adult.

4 Children playing with materials which had been selected by a teacher who was leading and guiding them towards the acquisition of certain facts.

Further observation and discussion followed, to try to determine which, if any, of these methods had the best chance of laying good foundations for the acquisition of mathematical concepts. The majority of teachers involved in the project felt that a combination of methods 2 and 3 gave young children the best chance to develop naturally while encouraging the least curious and extending those with more enquiring minds.

Many of the teachers taking part in these discussions said that since working with the project materials, they had become far more aware of the mathematics that is constantly going on in the normal activities of the class. By seeing these activities from the children's point of view they have been able to introduce relevant language, ideas and materials.

Other teachers felt that discussions about the stages of children's development towards acquiring mathematical concepts had helped to increase their own confidence in the methods they were already using.

Thus, the book makes many suggestions for the provision of activities and materials to stimulate mathematical thought whilst emphasising the role of the teacher in consolidating and extending the children's acquisition of mathematical concepts. It is not meant to be prescriptive in any way, but rather to help all those adults who work with young children to be aware of the many mathematical ideas which can be experienced by children in the course of their play.

The proportion of time that is spent in fostering these ideas will be determined by the circumstances of each group of children, bearing in mind that language development and social awareness are going on at the same time.

The effect of EME on the teachers is hard to evaluate, but some comments from them follow.

"Mathematics learning has been going on all around me but I've not always been aware of it. Now, by attending discussions I'm much more aware of what's happening. For example, talking about hair ribbons led to discussion of wide and narrow. It has reinforced the work I'm doing, jogged my memory about things I ought to be doing."

"In my own education mathematics was always separate, and although I did not want to treat it as a separate subject I felt I ought. I'm now confident that you help children develop mathematically by using opportunities as they arise in the child's work and/or play."

"Early Mathematical Experiences has been a great help. It's made me look at things afresh. I see mathematics where I didn't—especially dinner time activities."

"I think more about what mathematics means to the children. My approach has changed. I now take it from children's interest and experience."

"I think more from the child's point of view."

"I always liked stories and language, hated mathematics. I now know mathematics at nursery level can be done by talking with children. I now see opportunities when children are playing when I can intervene and help understanding."

"It's given me ideas. I have a more practical approach. I'm less keen on recording early. I'm looking for mathematics and opportunities to intervene."

"I'm more aware of the language I'm using. I approach mathematics through talking. I take nothing for granted. I assume no knowledge nor indeed accept the child understands the words he's using."

The teacher's role

The child and EME

Young children are very receptive, as can be seen from their delight in imitating and mastering such games as "Pat-a-cake, pat-a-cake" and repeating words from a well loved story, such as, "Who's been sitting in *my* chair?". Parents and older brothers and sisters are encouraged to try to teach them all manner of things—to walk, to talk, to throw a ball or bang a drum. However, it is not until a child has reached a certain stage in his physical and emotional development that these feats are accomplished. He may be told many times that *all* the milk from a jug cannot be poured into his cup, and finally accept this as a fact. Later, given the opportunity to play with water and pour from a jug into a cup over and over again, he begins to understand the reason for the fact. From this and many related experiences, the child is beginning to develop a concept of how liquids behave in various circumstances. Most adults take concepts such as this so much for granted that it is very difficult to imagine what life would be like without them; an over-turned bucket of potatoes is much easier to pick up than an overturned bucket of water!

The teacher of the very young tries to travel back with the children in her care to the point where these concepts are just beginning to be explored, taking nothing for granted. She needs to be a divergent thinker—seeing the various purposes in materials and therefore the possibilities. She gives them as many experiences as possible, not assuming, for example, that they understand the different properties of a piece of dough and a leaf. (Pull a lump of dough into small pieces and the pieces can be pressed together again, but pull a leaf apart and it is beyond repair.)

To a casual observer, the work of a teacher with a group of young children can look deceptively simple. The children appear to be absorbing ideas and facts without any deliberate attempt on the teacher's part to "teach" them. But it may not be realised just how much effort has been put in by the teacher to produce this state of affairs. Before setting out any activity she has had to consider:

1 The maturity of the group as a whole

2 The intellectual capacity of the particular children she has in mind

3 The *final* aim which this activity is leading towards

4 The amount of thinking and reasoning that the child will be called upon to exercise

5 The language development that might occur

6 The purely practical aspects of time, space and availability of materials and adult involvement.

It becomes obvious that without adult involvement, language development is unlikely to progress, but there are some occasions when children can be left to play on their own with, for example, sand or blocks. By repeating a simple action over and over again they are getting to understand some of the properties of that particular material. The sensitive teacher knows when a certain child is *not* ready to receive a new idea. She is also aware of children's need to regress. A feeling of insecurity, for any reason at all, is more easily dispelled by succeeding at something familiar, and thus regaining confidence.

On the other hand, it is not *always* best to wait for the child to make the first move. By waiting too long, a teacher may miss important opportunities for fostering his growth and development. Bruner (Bruner, J. S., *Towards a Theory of Instruction*, W. W. Norton & Co., New York, 1966.) suggests that the learning process can be encouraged by presenting work in a context that is appropriate to a child's level of understanding, and if he still appears "unready", the fault is more likely to lie in the way the experience was presented than in the child's immaturity. The role of the teacher is to provide a framework within which a child may progress and acquire as many skills as possible at his own level of understanding.

The immediate objective of any planned activity may be very obvious, like making a dish of cakes or a large collage picture of Humpty Dumpty or tidying the toy cupboard. The final aim which the teacher had in mind in each of these cases could well be mathematical: the one-to-one correspondence of the cakes to paper cases, the sorting of red pieces of material for Humpty Dumpty's shirt and the ideas of space, area and volume from packing toys into a cupboard.

As well as planning activities which lead towards definite objectives, teachers need to see the possibilities in games that children initiate themselves, and be ready to build on them. The teacher's idea of converting a large cardboard box into a doll's house may be abandoned if the first children to find it climb inside and decide it would make a very good boat.

These ideas are all elaborated in the chapters in part 2 and in the sections entitled "The teacher's role" examples of teachers' conversations with children are given. These have been chosen with a mathematical bias, and show the way children's ideas can be extended and built upon by the teacher who is aware of the possibilities.

Mathematics usually finds a natural place within the activities in the environment and cannot be treated as a separate subject. As an example of mathematics being brought in deliberately but unobtrusively, one teacher was preparing the harvest festival and decided on the story of the loaves and the fishes. She therefore made five stuffed fishes from old tights for the children to handle. Because she was mathematically aware, she made the fishes of different shapes and sizes and with different coloured fins, so providing many possible sorting activities.

One last point should be made. In every activity, it is the children's thinking, doing and speaking that is important. No great end-product may be apparent, and this is well summed up by a teacher who was asked for some children's work for an exhibition:

"I don't know what I'd exhibit. Today, for example, all I've got to show for what happened are some scruffy paper hats made by the children, but when I think of what went on in discussing, cutting circles, matching colours and shapes, it was terrific—*at the time!*"

Involvement of parents

Here is one teacher's view.

"I am quite sure we should do much more to educate parents. After all the child may only be with us for two and a half hours a day. We seem to have had some success in propagating the notion that an ability to recite the alphabet at five years does not mean that the child can read, but we have hardly started on the mathematics front. They need to know that the ability to recite a number sequence is not the same as having a concept of number.

"Communication is the first step and this depends on the local circumstances—some parents turn out very well to evening meetings. If they do not, perhaps a special notice board or individual notes could explain the special emphases of that week or month. I think it is time we were much more open about what we are doing and attempted to explain ourselves. Parents should know how far we are from a comprehensive learning theory and how difficult it is to find out exactly how children learn and what learning experiences give the optimum results.

"An evening spent getting the parents to do mental arithmetic in an unfamiliar notation should be fun and illuminating for the teachers as well as the parents." (See also R. Skemp, *The Psychology of Learning Mathematics*, Pelican, 1971, pp. 149–151.)
"We could explain the usefulness of playing games: ludo, snakes and ladders, tiddleywinks, cards.

"We could ask the parents to monitor their own language. How many times did you use the word 'two'—or whatever—this week? How much do you notice what is in the nursery? Ask your child why there is that collection of apparently random old boxes on the table. Try to find a suitable addition *with* him, for him to bring to school. This is much more effective than saying 'What did you do at school today?' which will probably bring a negative answer.

"Explain what experiences they can provide at home. Stress the importance of being a *parent* and not a teacher. Pushing the child along will produce the same attitude to maths as they probably have."

Whatever the school policy, the goodwill of parents is vital for the child's happiness and security in his first school. There are many reasons why not all parents can spend some time in the school; in extreme cases, the only contact will be at enrolment. Opportunity must be taken then to communicate not only the policy of the school but the value of play and adult conversation. In some areas, pastoral care is extended into the home through visits by the class teacher or a member of staff with special responsibility.

If parents have the opportunity, then involvement in the work of the school can be beneficial, not only to their own child. For example, parents might help, according to their own interests, with reading to a group, sewing, cooking or woodwork. In connection with such activities, the teacher may be able to point out possibilities of mathematical vocabulary. Many parents are anxious to learn and will enjoy a "maths session" if one can be set up at a suitable time. In this way, a real partnership between parents and teachers can be encouraged. Parents can also be very useful as an extra pair of hands during a walk and may learn from the teacher, for their own subsequent use, possibilities from the environment (What shapes do you notice?—narrow/wide roads, tall flats/squat bungalows, etc.).

Having debunked early prowess at number recitation, it is necessary for the teacher always to be available to satisfy the parent that progress is being made towards mathematical skills through such unlikely media as, for example, sand and water. It is a question of drawing attention to the number of concepts which have to be acquired before any arithmetical skills can be mastered and recorded.

Many authorities supply handouts on various subjects for parents of very young children starting school. Shown overleaf is an example of one from a Teachers' Centre.

Record keeping

There are almost as many different ways of keeping records as there are teachers keeping them. Records fall into three main categories: the medical-social type, those that a teacher keeps of the children in her care and those which may accompany a child through each stage of his education, indicating his academic attainment at certain ages.

When children first start school, the medical-social information may seem most important, and many parents are willing to co-operate. Experienced teachers, social and welfare staff then help to fill in some of the gaps from their own observations and personal contacts.

Getting ready for Maths

You are probably helping your child get ready for Mathematics in many ways, maybe without realising it! Here are some of the many activities that you can do *with your child* which will help.

Laying the table—counting, getting the knives in the right place, etc.
Going shopping—handling money, counting items in basket.
Dressing and undressing—sorting clothes into piles.
Helping with cooking—weighing, measuring.
Playing with water—at bathtime, washing up.
Tidying away toys.
Left and *right* games.
Spotting shapes (circles, squares, etc.) colours, comparing sizes, etc., whether at home or on walks.

No doubt you can think of many more. The important thing is that you help your child to get hold of the basic ideas of Maths, such as sorting, matching and comparing. By sharing an activity with your child and by talking to him, you can begin to introduce the correct "Mathematical" words such as big and small, few and many, longest and shortest and so on. But don't turn it into a lesson. All these things can be done incidentally as a part of day to day events. Please note. The BBC Schools TV Programme "You and Me" (Tuesdays at 2 p.m.) is about "early mathematics" and you may enjoy watching it as a change from "Watch with Mother"!

A teacher's own record, which she keeps to help her monitor and plan the day by day progression of her group of children, is quite a different matter and may change from year to year as she looks back on courses of action which were or were not successful. Faced with a new group of children she begins "sorting" and her first criteria are most likely to be:

1 Those with whom I can communicate

2 Those with whom I can't communicate.

Very soon these wide divisions can be broken down into sub-sets such as:

1 a) children who can communicate verbally
  b) children who by their actions show that they understand my speech, but do not communicate in words

2 Children who do not understand my speech because:
  a) they speak and understand a different language
  b) they have failed to learn to communicate in any language
  c) they have physical defects

Although a teacher may not actually write down this rather complicated scheme, it will certainly be in her mind as she plans the activities for her group of children, and it is at this point that individual records become important.

Of course, these records will be concerned with manual and physical dexterity, social habits and language development, as well as with the acquisition of mathematical ideas.

Teachers of very young children have always planned and organised an integrated day so they realise that mathematics cannot be separated from the rest of the programme. Nevertheless, they see children beginning to absorb mathematical ideas which need very little knowledge of language.

For example:
A child recognises his own coat:
a) by colour or style
b) by its position on a row of pegs in relation to other coats
c) because it is hanging next to a symbol which he recognises as his sign.

From observations such as this, teachers begin to assess a child's intellectual development and can record his progress under various headings, in their own particular style.

An example of one method is given here:

Sorting: can classify objects according to likeness.
Ordering: can put things in order of size.
Matching: can match two sets of objects.
Pattern: can repeat a given pattern.

These headings, if put at the top of separate columns, cards or pages, could be filled in with a detail and date if appropriate, from general observation.

For example:

JOHN BLOGGS			
Sorting	*Ordering*	*Matching*	*Pattern*
3 Colours 8/9/75	4 dolls 28/6/75	Cups to Saucers 10/10/75	Alternate beads 10/11/75
4 shapes 18/1/76	Nesting boxes 9/9/76		3 shapes in sequence 1/2/76

It soon becomes obvious that language development goes hand in hand with the acquisition of mathematical ideas, and the vocabulary concerned with the concepts of comparison, shape, space and number will play an increasing part.

As children's communication with adults develops, further details may be added to the record such as the understanding and use of comparative words for length, weight, volume and number—bigger/smaller, longer/shorter, more/less, a lot/a little. Children should also be acquiring a vocabulary of spatial words, such as up/down, in front of/behind, above/beneath, all of which can be noted.

Some teachers are responsible for a large number of young children and the task of keeping records must not take up more time than the results justify. Most of the stages mentioned can be recorded from the children's natural play and their talk with one another, as well as with adults. At this early stage, it is not possible to say that a child has "done" matching, for example. However, several entries under that heading, showing his success with different materials such as cups to saucers, milk bottles to straws, buttons to buttonholes and tins to lids can indicate his progression and readiness for more sophisticated activities.

If there appears to be a lack of progression in a certain area, the teacher is able to plan ahead and give the child more experience in that particular area. For example, a child who lacks skill in sorting may be asked to help tidy the toy box, or the bricks according to their size, or the crayons according to colour.

A number of teachers have found it useful to make diary entries about children, noting their day to day activities.

But what about the information that is passed on to another teacher? She may be in the next room or the next school, but will certainly want to know something about the group of children she is taking on. It has long been the practice to take groups of children to meet their new teachers and see their new classrooms. Some teachers think it would be just as helpful for the new teachers to meet their next classes while they are still in the nursery or kindergarten. In this way the teacher would see many of the activities that the children are being encouraged to take part in and make her own decisions about their capabilities (as a group). Children with particular interests or failings could be pointed out to her and the records that had been kept could be shown to her. Together, they could decide which information would be most helpful in providing continuity of experience for the children.

If this personal contact is not possible, then written notes must be relied upon and many local authorities are experimenting with various cards and lists which will convey vital information in the most economical way. Although a lengthy personal record may give a better all-round picture of a child, the new teacher who wishes to find out which child is liable to have an asthma attack or can already count in twos and fives, really needs a quick reference chart. For this reason, as far as mathematics is concerned, it may be better to make a summary check list, which picks out some of the points which have already been recorded. The following is one that might be useful.

It gives suggestions of activities that would demonstrate a child's progress in the acquisition of various concepts.

1) *Sorting*: can sort a collection of ten objects (not all alike) and discuss how.

2) *Ordering*: given five crayons or pencils of different lengths, can order them according to their length.

3) *Matching*: given five cubes in a line and a pile of toy cars, can match a car to each cube.

4) *Comparisons*: given two balls of different sizes, can point out the differences, i.e. "This one is bigger" or "This one is smaller", "This one is heavier" or "This one is lighter".

5) *Shape recognition*: given a miscellaneous collection of triangles, squares and circles, can name them and also recognise them when, for example, the square is placed on one of its corners and the triangles are not necessarily isosceles.

6) *Spatial ordering*: given a string of six different coloured beads or six different coloured cubes in a line, can copy this by selection from a pile.

7) *Topology*: can carry out instructions to place a book "behind", "beside", "in front of" or "above" another object.

It is not necessary to use exactly the same materials as those suggested—for instance a cherry could be *matched* to the top of each cake during a cooking session, instead of a car to a cube. The important point is that it is *one-to-one correspondence*, and if there are more cherries than cakes, the surplus cherries will be left in their jar.

Two examples of record-keeping are given below. These have actually been used by teachers. They are not reproduced by EME as the perfect answers to a difficult problem but simply as a basis for discussion.

Example 1

Below is a sample record which could be filled in with a tick when a child has reached this particular stage. As these ideas can develop through all the various activities of the classroom, the list has not been tied to any particular one. For example, the ordering could be of dolls, bricks, buckets, leaves, animals, children, books, etc. etc. It is in no way meant to be a 4+ leaving examination! It is, in fact, for the teacher's own use; the criteria are not sharply defined, but she will know what *she* means.

Example 2

The record form on pages 22 and 23 brings some mathematical concepts out into the open. Again, it would be a matter for local discussion just when a tick was placed against any item or whether some note might be added at the side. The entry for Routes clearly has a locally-understood meaning and no doubt + and − are abbreviations for the teacher to remind her that the children may be sorting sets rather than using the abstract symbols themselves.

1 Can sort a variety of articles, picking out sameness and difference.	....
2 Can sort a variety of objects into categories suggested by teacher.	
a) colour	....
b) size	....
c) shape	....
d) other	....
3 Can choose and explain his own sorting categories.	....
4 Understands some comparative words.	....
5 Can order three or more objects visually by size.	....
6 Understands: inside	....
outside	....
on	....
in front of	....
behind	....
next to	....

(Example 2)

RECORD OF PROGRESS

NAME .... Date of Birth ....

Concepts of Size
Big/small	bigger/smaller	wide/narrow
a lot/a little	more/less	long/short

Concepts of Position
up/down	in front/behind	level/upright	back/front
above/beneath	left/right	open/close	side/round about
top/bottom	across/up and down		

Comparison   quantities without counting

Attributes   can isolate   1 attribute—positive/negative   can isolate   3 attributes—positive/negative
can isolate   2 attributes—positive/negative   can isolate   4 attributes—positive/negative

Routes   2.   3.   4.

Patterns   bead threading/shape sticking/drawing

Matching/naming   colours   pictures   shapes   1 to 1

Seriate by size   squares
triangles
circles
other objects

Grouping
make groups	0 to 5	5 to 10
name groups	0 to 5	5 to 10
count groups	0 to 5	5 to 10
draw numerals	0 to 5	5 to 10
recognise numerals	0 to 5	5 to 10
+	0 to 5	5 to 10
−	0 to 5	5 to 10

(Example 2)

RECORD OF PROGRESS

NAME .... Date of Birth ....

	Always	Usually	Sometimes	Never
Uses pencil well				
Uses scissors well				
Draws writing patterns				
Recognises own name				
Helps with activities				
Keeps himself occupied				
Understands simple instructions quickly				
Talks freely to strangers				
Has good memory for people/places				
Dresses himself				
Puts on own shoes				

	Term 1	Term 2	Term 3
Concentration			
Retention			
Attitude to peers			
Attitude to adults			
Observation			
Speech/vocabulary			
Use of sentences/phrases			
Answering questions			
Listening to stories			

Interests

Where's all this leading to?

The topic chapters are mainly concerned with concepts—sorting, ordering, matching and comparisons in particular have recurred frequently. Why? First of all, the acqusition of such fundamental ideas is part of the children's birthright: helped on by relevant experiences, the children will come to them naturally. (It is a pity that it is easier to demonstrate deficiencies than achievements: it is all too obvious when a child goes to school at five having been deprived of fruitful conversation and experiences.)

But apart from this "birthright" aspect, it might also be of interest to look briefly at "where it's all leading to". To start with a good old-fashioned example, sooner or later children will need to be able to perform simple calculations such as $8 + 5 = 13$. They should not be encouraged to write such equations until they have had many experiences: when they know that 8 apples and 5 more apples gives a total of 13 apples, that 8 oranges and 5 more oranges gives 13 oranges, that 8 miscellaneous bits of fruit (of all shapes and sizes) and 5 more bits gives altogether 13 bits—that in fact *it doesn't matter what things you have*, as long as there are 8 things and 5 things, the total is 13 things, only at this moment does it make sense to abstract the notion $8 + 5 = 13$.

Handling objects is a prerequisite to the addition of numbers, and so immediately we are dealing with *sets*. The idea of a number itself, for example 5, is also abstracted from many experiences. To be really familiar with 5, the following are necessary:

1) To be able to recognise 5 things and to realise that they remain 5 even if they are moved around the table (this is called "the invariance of number of objects in a set").

Experiences leading to this idea can certainly be started in the nursery. There is a sad story of a child who couldn't agree there were 5 ducks as there "wasn't one in the middle". (See *Towards Number* p. 96.)

2) To understand the "story of 5":
$$5 = 4 + 1$$
$$5 = 3 + 2$$
$$5 = 1 + 1 + 3$$
etc.

This comes from many experiences with sets of objects and partitioning them in different ways, e.g. toy animals can have a moveable fence across their field.

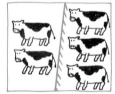

3) To know 5 as having its place in the sequence 1, 2, 3, 4, 5, 6, 7, ... between 4 and 6. This involves the idea of *ordering* numbers, and in turn this is preceded by many other simple *ordering* experiences, objects according to size, weight, length, etc.

4) To know that 5 is greater than 4 ($5 > 4$), it is also necessary to be able to make *comparisons*. "There are more

animals here *than* there" builds up to the idea "how many more?" and so to $5 > 4$, $5 = 4 + 1$, etc.

5) To be able to count to 5, absolutely confidently and right every time. This involves *matching*, because counting is simply a special case of matching.

Returning to the sum $8 + 5 = 13$, we have so far only dealt with "5" (and similarly "8"), but even the understanding of this involves a lot of earlier work with ideas of

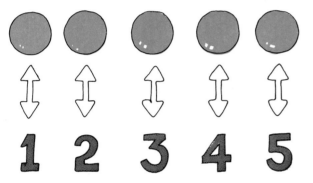

sorting, matching, etc. as detailed above, which can be started at this stage of education.

Beyond this level, the children will have to understand "place-value": that "13" stands for one in the tens place and 3 in the units place. They will also have to make the abstraction from sets to numbers mentioned above which makes sense of "plus" as an operation and the idea of equivalence before they can use the symbol " = " with meaning. The point being made here is that a sound appreciation of the basic concepts described in the book is essential for the understanding (and so even enjoyment) of later mathematics. Our "sum" is, of course just one example; and it is not difficult to trace in a similar way other mathematical skills to their early roots, and not only numerical ones.

One vast area which has been neglected in the past is that of spatial awareness and relationships. Some children begin by being markedly more advanced in spatial ideas rather than numerical ones, and while things may level out later, some such children undoubtedly have special talents leading towards the arts (including mathematics!). It has been a shame in the past that such children have had the enthusiasm knocked out of them by insistence that primary "mathematics" meant just "arithmetic". These days are happily past, and children are encouraged to think purposefully and creatively on the spatial side as well as the numerical one.

The appreciation of properties of shapes is a necessary prerequisite for the study of geometry. This is concerned with manipulating shapes and using operations such as translation, rotation and reflection.

Translation: this is the single movement of an object without turning it.

Rotation: this is moving an object through an angle.

Reflection: this is replacing an object by its "image" as if it had been reflected in a mirror.

On these three simple "movements", much of school geometry can be based. With the very young child, first steps may be taken with a frieze of potato prints, experimenting by turning things round (including oneself) and literally looking at mirrors and the effect of seeing things in them. (See also the books by Marion Walter, published by Andre Deutsch, *Annette* (1971), *Make a Bigger Puddle* (1971) and *Another, Another, Another and More* (1975).

Measurement is another later activity. Whatever is being measured—length, area, weight, volume, etc.— there is a progression of ideas. First measures are made informally, with handspans, bags of sand, building bricks, etc., and the "standard" (gram, metre, etc.) is only introduced when its need is felt, which may well be at junior rather than infant level. All the time the approximate nature of *all* measurement has to be stressed. This progression is facilitated by early experiences such as "this ribbon is longer than that one", "the book is three hands long", "this stone feels heavier than that one": again, we are right back where it all starts, with early mathematical experiences.

Before "standard" measurement has any meaning, a child must have acquired the relevant concept of invariance (see p. 7). The invariance of number has been referred to above. The invariance of length, for example, implies that a strip of wood remains the same length no matter how it is moved around so long as a bit is not snapped off. Young children may well agree that two strips are the same length when put side-by-side but then insist that one is longer when it is moved sideways. At this stage measurement in centimetres is quite valueless. It is impossible to *teach* invariance in the sense of trying to explain it to children, but it is possible to provide a wide range of experiences from which children will eventually acquire the idea. Young children learn more by handling things than being told about them.

For the older children, debate will continue on the balance between concepts and skills (neither is much use without the other), but at EME level it is clear that concepts have absolute priority. There is so much to learn before the simplest calculations can have any meaning, that the idea of "sums for the very young child" is ludicrous. But the foundations are crucial for later work and these are being laid through the EME activities.

The National Curriculum

"What happens next after EME?" will now be discussed briefly in more detail. The short immediate answer to "Where's all this leading to?" is the National Curriculum in Mathematics for England and Wales. This is the mathematical part of the statutory curriculum for children aged 5 to 16 in state schools.

There are 14 Attainment Targets (Such as Using and Applying Mathematics; Number; Measure) and each target has 10 levels of difficulty.

EME is of course designed to help children forward *at their present level* and is in no sense for cramming towards the National Curriculum. All the same, it is good to be aware that EME is laying the foundations for future work. Accordingly, Level 1 of each Attainment Target is given in this section, together with a few examples from this book. These illustrate the EME activities which are needed for the subsequent attainment of the Targets at their initial levels.

Attainment Target 1: using and applying mathematics

Pupils should use number, algebra and measures in practical tasks, in real-life problems, and to investigate within mathematics itself.

Statements of Attainment, Level 1 Pupils should:
  use materials provided for a task
  talk about own work and ask questions
  make predictions based on experience

p.53 Which one is heavier?
      They are both the same heavy

p.48 Can you make a bridge with this plank so that I can reach you? Is it long enough?

p.50 Is this castle larger than that one?

Attainment Target 2: number

Pupils should read and understand number and number notation.

Statements of Attainment, Level 1 Pupils should:
  count, read, write and order numbers to at least 10;
  know that the size of a set is given by the last number in the count
  understand the conservation of number.

pp.99-107 Towards Number

      In Chapter 12, there are many examples of counting and ordering numbers.

p. 10   Cardinal number of a set.

p. 67   Counting birthday cards, fingers etc.

p. 135   Busy streets: counting vehicles by matching.

p. 40   How many beads will fit inside that box?

p. 113   How many blue cubes do you need to build a cube the same size as the red cube?

Attainment Target 3: number

Pupils should understand number operations (addition, subtraction, multiplication and division) and make use of appropriate methods of calculation.

Statements of Attainment, Level 1   Pupils should:
add or subtract using objects, where the numbers involved are no greater than 10.

p. 56   We need another knife — I've only got two and I need three.

In Chapter 12 there is follow-up work for addition and subtraction, e.g. (p.156) 'The bees' and (p.158) 'The monkeys'.

p. 67   Blowing out candles on the cake.

p. 73   Fiona made four biscuits ... "I couldn't give one to Daddy because there weren't enough ..."

Attainment Target 4: number

Pupils should estimate and approximate in number.

Statements of Attainment, Level 1   Pupils should:
give a sensible estimate of a small number of objects (up to 10).

Attainment Target 5: number/algebra

Pupils should recognise and use patterns, relationships and sequences, and make generalisations.

Statements of Attainment, Level 1   Pupils should:
copy, continue and devise repeating patterns represented by objects/apparatus and one-digit numbers.

p. 89   Can you make a necklace the same as mine?

p. 92   Printing: the activities suggested help the children to focus their work on copying and devising patterns.

p. 115   Paragraph headed 'Patterns and sequences'.

Attainment Targets 6 and 7: algebra

Nothing specific required at Level 1 in the National Curriculum.

Attainment Target 8: measures

Pupils should estimate and measure quantities, and appreciate the approximate nature of measurement.

Statements of Attainment, Level 1 Pupils should:
  compare and order objects without measuring, and use appropriate language.

p. 47 Do you think John's tower is taller than yours?

p. 49 Which piece of paper is the right size to cover the front of this box?

p. 70 This length fits round my head.

Attainment Target 9: using and applying mathematics

Pupils should use shape and space and handle data in practical tasks, in real-life problems, and to investigate within mathematics itself.

Statements of Attainment, Level 1 Pupils should:
  use materials provided for a task
  talk about own work and ask questions
  make predictions based on experience.

p. 110 (Matthew and Clare trying to make a tower 'the size of Clare')
  We need some more bricks, I reckon we must put some more of those on.
  It is too tall — now take some off
  That is just the right size now.

Attainment Target 10: shape and space

Pupils should recognise and use the properties of two-dimensional and three-dimensional shapes.

Statements of Attainment, Level 1 Pupils should:
  sort 3-0 and 2-0 shapes
  build with 3-0 solid shapes and draw 2-0 shapes and describe them.

Chapter 1, especially pp. 39 – 43

p. 43 Emma choosing painting paper: "I think I'll have a square one — no, a triangle."

pp. 134 , 135 Looking for shapes in the Environment.

Attainment Target 11: shape and space

Pupils should recognise location and use transformations in the study of space.

Statements of Attainment, Level 1 Pupils should:
  state a position using prepositions such as on, inside, above, under, behind, next to, etc.
  give and understand instructions for moving along a line.

p. 11 "We've made a bridge. The cars go over the bridge and the boats go under."

p. 36 Following instructions: "the box is in the cupboard on the middle shelf next to the crayons".

p. 44 Matthew picked up a triangular piece of paper, held it up on one vertex, looked at it for a moment, then said "It's a triangle, isn't it? But it's upside down."

Attainment Target 12: handling data

Pupils should collect, record and process data.

Statements of Attainment, Level 1   Pupils should:
   select criteria for sorting a set of objects and apply consistently.

p. 102 Many suggestions for sorting, e.g. doll's house furniture to be placed in particular rooms. Sometimes the children themselves form sets, e.g. those wearing/not wearing red sandals.

Attainment Target 13: handling data

Pupils should represent and interpret data.

Statements of Attainment, Level 1   Pupils should:
   record with real objects or drawings, and comment about the result
   create simple mapping diagrams showing relationships; read and interpret them.

p. 37   Lining up. (The 'real objects' at this level are often the children themselves).

p. 104 The children place a symbol or name tag on a bottle of milk at the beginning of the day to label their own.

Attainment Target 14: handling data

Pupils should understand, estimate and calculate probabilities.

Statements of Attainment, Level 1   Pupils should:
   recognise possible outcomes of simple random events.

At this level, questioning will be extremely simple, e.g. "Do you think it will snow to-morrow?" or "Will the new baby be a girl or a boy?"

p. 126   Tunnels. Children who are just watching can be encouraged to discuss who they think will come out first.

Part 2
EME Topic Chapters

Introduction to part 2

The second part of this book consists of 12 "topics" or areas of activity. It must be emphasised that these topics are in no sense "graded" in order of difficulty and there are many ways of using them within the school organisation.

A few general points may be kept in mind.

Apparatus, toys and games can all be useful, but none are essential.

For *Outdoor activities* and *The Environment*, safety of the children is paramount. Before exploring with the children beyond the school gates, it is wise for the teacher to familiarise herself with the area and ensure that plenty of adults are available for any expedition.

With *Rhymes and Stories*, don't be tempted to over-do the mathematics and feel that it must be dragged in on every occasion.

For *Passage of Time*, the object is to give the children a feeling for time rather than teaching how to tell the time with a clock, which comes later.

Above all, don't treat mathematics as a separate subject but find it among the interests and activities of the children.

1 Space and Shape

Introduction

Two themes are discussed below—*space* and *shape*. It is difficult to define boundaries between the two, as shapes take up space. *Shapes* are all around us; regular and irregular, constant or changing. Young children, as they explore the world about them, need not only to look at shapes, but to feel them also—the straight edge, flat surface, rounded sides, sharp points. They can experiment with the way each one behaves; rounded shapes roll, those with flat surfaces will usually stand still. They can try fitting shapes together, side by side, on top of, underneath or inside each other.

As for *space*, we usually have enough for ourselves and so are less aware of it. But squash us into a rush hour bus and we are suddenly aware of just how much space we need and how much others take up! Children squashed together in a Story Corner soon complain if there is "not enough room", and often need our suggestion in order to rearrange themselves more comfortably.

It is easy to forget that space exists above, as well as to the side, and children can make use of this space as they play with balls, kites, balloons or bubbles.

"I can't reach it."

Because our bodies are jointed we are able to bend our limbs to fit various shapes and though we do not, of course, "fill less space", we can make more effective use of the space available. We bend to sit on chairs, hold arms and legs in when squashed into a small floor space, or bend down to pass through a low archway. Young children need plenty of freedom to explore and develop their

"I'm squashed!"

33

physical skills, and by providing a wide range of equipment we offer both challenge and opportunity for them to do so.

We tend to arrange objects to make the most effective use of space available. Chairs and tables might be moved to alter the shape of the usable floor space, and children often enjoy arranging and rearranging furniture in a doll's house or Home Corner, as well as being practically involved in organisation of furniture and equipment in the classroom.

They need to stretch up to reach high shelves or place yet another brick on a tall tower. Though most materials are arranged at eye-level, it is sometimes interesting to suspend art work or mobiles from strings across the room to provide variety of height and perspective.

Some shapes fit together readily, as we know from packing bags or putting things away in cupboards. Some are specifically designed to fit inside each other, or, like clothes, to fit or cover something else.

The environment provides plenty of material for discussions of shapes—shapes which fit together, which look alike, which grow or change. Not all children will have had the opportunity to grow plants and flowers from seeds or bulbs, or are encouraged to notice and discuss the development and changes that take place. Not all will have seen a bud open to reveal a leaf or a flower, or will have watched the transformation from spawn to tadpole to frog.

Example
Emily (3.4) and her teacher were looking at bulbs.
Emily: Look, they're growing.
Teacher: I have some bulbs growing at home.

Emily: Me as well. Look, this is bigger. It's coming out the top. (Pointing to the shoot) That's coming out the side. (Pointing to the other bulb)

Growing things

The child's experience is predominantly of handling and using three-dimensional solids. Two-dimensional shapes are encountered in painting, printing, taking rubbings, in pattern or design, or in covering one surface of a three-dimensional object. The child who uses a cylinder to print with will soon discover that what he produces with each end are circles—he might even find out that they are circles of the same size!

It is through our awareness of the importance of the child's freedom to explore and experiment in space and shape, and our willingness to encourage and stimulate these activities, that each child is able to experience the variety from which he might generalise later.

Possible developments

Movement and space

Children will begin to experience space as they move and explore. Most children will be used to moving, but may not have had opportunity to move freely in large open spaces or in busy crowded rooms, and in both cases may need time and encouragement before they will feel happy to play freely.

Children may often have "too much" space, but there are also times when they experience "too little". Very often young children would rather be uncomfortably squashed than move from their story-teller or part with the shiny, if cramped, new car! Nevertheless, they may very well be experimenting with their own body shape to make it "as small as possible" or "fit this car", though quite unaware that they are doing so.

There are many ways in which children might be said to be experiencing space through their own movement. There are also times when the teacher might legitimately focus their attention on the way in which they move, encouraging awareness of their movement and introducing vocabulary to describe it. It would, of course, be futile, if not dangerous, to stop a child balanced perilously at the top of a climbing frame to ask how he came to arrive at that position—the fact that he has overcome the self-imposed challenge is an achievement in itself.

The teacher can, however, provide a range and variety of challenges inherent in the large equipment which is put out for the children to use. Afterwards the different problems that were encountered and differences that were noticed might be discussed.

The teacher can introduce new vocabulary and ideas of position and direction through working with groups of children in movement sessions, and often these might be reinforced by discussions with the children as they handle equipment in their play.

These are some of the activities in which this experience might occur.

General play
Outdoors: climbing, balancing, running, swinging, steering, catching, jumping, skipping.

Indoors: moving amongst equipment, setting out equipment, finding space in which to play, playing in restricted space—Home Corner, Story Corner.

The teacher might set out different pieces and combinations of large apparatus, or site the apparatus differently.

The children might be helped to take an increasingly responsible role in the care and organisation of equipment.

Play with small apparatus
For example, the children can play with balls, bats, skittles, shuttle-cocks, balloons, paper aeroplanes, kites, bubble

pipes. The use of apparatus might be discussed and other ways of using it suggested.

> Throwing the ball up higher than the top of the barrel. See if you can roll the ball between the skittles.

Vocabulary: higher than – further than – nearer than – over – across – between – to – up – down.

Group and ring games

Farmer's in his den, Ring a' ring o' roses, In and out the bluebells, What's the time, Mr Wolf? and other group games and activity rhymes can be introduced and the relevant vocabulary discussed.

Movement session

This might include movement to music or rhythms, and games like "musical statues".

At this stage body awareness is important. A group of children will need their teacher to describe their body movements in words. It is difficult for young children to move as they are told to, and they may need someone to demonstrate the meaning of moving "backwards" or "sideways", for instance. It might be that a child who has achieved some understanding of the terms will sometimes be the "model".

Initially, simple instructions might be given. Run. Stop. Jump up and down. As children become more familiar with these, then challenges might be varied and increased. Make a pointed shape high up.

Vocabulary: high – low – near – far – up – down – forwards – backwards – sideways – quick – slow – pointed – twisted – straight – curled – above – below – as tall/small/wide/long/ as possible – around – in between – next to – in front of – behind.

Early ideas of position, distance and length

Change of position

Ideas of change of position can be introduced when:

> talking about walks or journeys, perhaps to school, to auntie's, to the bus stop, etc.;
> inviting older children to trace a route they have taken on a simple picture—for instance, a house might be drawn as a starting point and school as the journey's end;
> making models of the school, the street and the classroom, and adding model cars, animals and people;
> using the doll's house to discuss the position of furniture or doll's house people.

The classroom or playground gives a good basis for discussion. Provision of model houses, trees, etc. for a model of the immediate environment might provide insight into the child's stage of thinking.

Example

One wet morning we were discussing how far we had walked to school in the rain.

Jason (4.6): I just have to come round two corners and I'm at school.

Position

There are occasions when children might need to locate objects or positions, either by following instructions, "the box is in the cupboard on the middle shelf next to the crayons", or by describing for themselves where they last saw the teddy bear. There is some skill in defining a position adequately to another person.

Experience of position can occur in the following activities:

Movement session Children may follow instructions involving a reference point, e.g. behind the white line. This occurs in many improvised games.

Constructional play Children may occasionally want to talk about the construction of the model itself—"We put the window in the front wall near the door"—or the position of things within it—"The man is standing outside the field: he's a long way from the house."

Gardening For example, the children can plant seeds or bulbs—"in a row", "far apart".

Vocabulary: behind – in front – next to – inside – outside – on – on top of – underneath – in between – into – under – above – below – over.

Spatial order

An obvious example of spatial order is "lining up" when children will often remember their position as, for example, behind Sally and in front of John.

"You pushed in!"

In more deliberate activities, children might be asked to copy a sequence of cards, a line of colours or a row of beads with a matched sequence of their own. It is not obvious to a young child that this is best achieved by taking a starting point and working systematically along a line. It is even more difficult if the sequence is arranged in a ring, perhaps to form a bracelet.

Some other opportunities for spatial ordering:

Lining up: queues, taking turns.

Tidying up: paint next to brushes, observing books in rows, coats on pegs, boxes on shelves.

Copying sequence: printing, painting, cards, cubes, etc.

Modelling: imitating a series of houses, cars or people.

Model villages, railway, car tracks, etc. "Which part of the train will reach the tunnel first?" "Which carriage will come out after the red one?"

Vocabulary: near – far away – nearer/nearest – further/furthest – beside – next to – in front of – behind – in between – before – after – first – last.

Lines

Constructing a straight line can be a difficult task even for a seven- or eight-year-old. A young child may, for instance, when given model trees to place in a straight line from A to B, produce something like 1 if the tray is rectangular, 2 if the tray is circular.

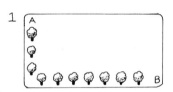 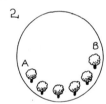

Children may need to make a line of individual objects when tidying away, for example, pots of paint or empty milk bottles. They might need help to plant seeds or bulbs in rows or to place houses in a line on a model street, or perhaps to arrange chairs in line for a game.

Discussion can arise of things that are placed in rows outside school: houses, trees, lamp posts, cars. One might, for example, suggest "sighting", by standing at one end of some railings to see the other railings in line.

Vocabulary: line – straight – curved – row – in front – behind – next to.

Distance and length

Constructing straight lines by placing objects immediately "next door to" each other is a very early step towards ideas of measurement of length. Placing a line of similar cubes along one side of a table, children begin to see that the side of the table is about the same length as that number of cubes.

When it comes to distance, the young child is strongly influenced by his own limited experiences. He might, for example, be familiar with the journey from home to auntie's and believe auntie's house to be close to home, whilst the unfamiliar, but shorter, journey to the dentist will be "a long way away".

Children are also influenced by the way things look. Two houses might be thought closer together when a fence is placed to join them. Fred on top of the hill might be thought nearer to Bill at the bottom, than Bill at the bottom is to Fred, simply because of the slope! Early experience of play with cars or toys on slopes, hills and stairs may be valuable, both for the children and for providing insight into their stage of thinking.

"You come down to me—it's not so far!"

Experiences of distance and length might be involved in some of the following:

Constructional play: blocks in rows, perhaps to make sides of buildings, roadways or just longer lines.

Printing: lines of shapes "next door to" each other, variety of shapes, hand prints, etc.

Model farms, etc.: discussion of distance between objects.

Slopes: moving on slopes themselves—"How many paces up, how many down?" etc.

Seesaw: Are children at either end always the same distance apart?

Lining up: children themselves make a row, perhaps against the wall or between reference points, e.g. "from the door to the red table".

Patterns: playing with pieces of string cut to the same length.

Vocabulary: near to – far away from – next to – along – between – line – row – straight – curved – edge – length – as long as – shorter than – nearer to – further from.

Measurement

The capacity to estimate length or height is a skill which is only gradually acquired. The child who makes a perceptual comparison, when asked to build a tower the same height as another, has achieved a new stage in his thinking. Later he might try to "level off" the heights, or make a rough measure by adjusting the space between his hands or using a stick or piece of string.

The teacher may suggest a more challenging comparison of measurement when the towers or constructions are to be made from different levels (one on the floor, one on the table) or of differently sized blocks or sections, which eliminates the possibility of one-to-one matching.

Vocabulary: shorter than – taller than – longer than – same length – wider than – narrower than.

Three-dimensional shape

Children begin to abstract properties of objects and to identify shapes, not only by looking but also by handling or using them. In their play they are able to experiment with a range of materials of all shapes and sizes.

The adult might be tempted to assume that any child who handles an object is having experience of three-dimensional shape, but is the child waving a ball above his head (awaiting the imminent arrival of his imaginary space-ship) aware of the ball as a sphere or as a space-ship?

It is obviously not always appropriate to ask: "What shape is it?" Indeed, the label may not be so important as discussing "What would happen if you . . .?" (roll it, stand it on this slope, try to stand it upside down, etc.). Similarities and differences between shapes of objects can also be discussed.

Whilst always being sensitive to the child's thinking as he plays, there are times when it might be appropriate to talk about the properties of the materials he handles.

How shapes behave
Constructional play can give experience of how shapes behave.

Roll plastic bottles, buckets—do they roll in the same way?

Discuss "what happened when . . .?" (a cylinder was placed on slope, etc.).

Occasionally the teacher may introduce slopes, rough surfaces, blankets, etc. during play with bricks, as well as providing an assortment of other shapes, such as cylinders.

The teacher might discuss with the children oddments in the junk box and other collections, for example from the environment. What are they usually used for? Do they stand/hang up/roll, etc.?

Vocabulary: curved – straight – pointed – angles – edge – flat – coiled – spiral – rolls – rough – smooth.

Properties
The teacher might make a "feely" bag. This game creates a need for the children to describe tactile properties.

At other times visual similarities and differences of objects might be discussed. This will be involved in sorting activities.

Opportunities may be taken to talk with children about anything and everything—apparatus, flowers, etc.

What do they look like? What else looks like that? Is it the same? How is it different?

Vocabulary: round – straight – curved – pointed – looks like.

Matching shapes
Children often make spontaneous discoveries when using the range of materials and natural objects provided. The teacher might encourage this exploration. Find another one that looks like this. Is it the same? What is different about it? What else has the same shape? Let's make a tower with all the shapes that look like this one.

Vocabulary: looks the same – looks like – different.

Shapes that fit together
For example, blocks, junk models, furniture (e.g. stacking chairs), goods in the shop on shelves, collage work, jigsaws, babushka dolls give experience of fitting together.

The teacher can provide a variety of shapes to be used and might talk with the children about the choice of shapes combined.

Stimulate three-dimensional representation by asking the children to copy shapes, real or seen in pictures, particularly familiar things.

Vocabulary: fits – balances.

Using space

Apparatus can be put into boxes or drawers, bags or suitcases can be packed, and the class and Home Corner areas can be tidied. The children can climb into large apparatus, fill trucks or trailers with bricks, sand or toys, or pour sand, jelly or plaster into moulds.
Children are often content to use space inefficiently.

> Can you put the puzzle away so that the lid will fit?
> How many beads will fit inside that box? Encourage rough estimation ("this handful") and check.

"All of my toys fitted in."   "Mine didn't."

Vocabulary: inside – outside – full – empty – half full – more – less – fewer – not so many.

Altering shapes

By changing shapes children can have experience of observing and talking about those characteristics which change and those which stay the same. Some of these changes are reversible, others not. In some, the children use the same amount of a material to mould it into different forms, leading towards the idea of invariance. Some opportunities for altering shapes are given below.

Folding: paper, material, clothes, cloths, etc.
Rolling: material, napkins, clay, dough, etc.
Stretching: elastic, material, clay, dough, etc.
Modelling: clay, dough, plasticine, papier mâché, etc.
Squeezing: clay, dough, plasticine, cloth, etc.
Opening out: boxes, packets, etc.
Pouring: liquid, sand, etc. to assume shape of different containers.
Growing things: plants, flowers, animals.
Chopping and shredding
Baking: mixing ingredients, dough rising, etc.

> What happened when you folded/rolled that paper?
> What did it look like?
> Fold that paper until it looks as small as possible.
> Open out that box and see what it looks like.

Example

Jamie (4.3) was making Christmas decorations. He cut a triangle from folded paper and opening it out, said: "Look, I've made a square!"

Vocabulary: longer – shorter – rounded – flat – fatter – thinner – curved – straight.

Two-dimensional shape

Children live in a three-dimensional world. Sooner or later, however, they will start exploring flat and other surfaces (of boxes, balls and so on), looking at pictures in books, playing with picture cards, and so become interested in things in two dimensions. A box is three dimensional but its sides are two dimensional. The covering of surfaces has been included in this section.

Three-dimensional to two-dimensional

The transition from three-dimensional to two-dimensional shapes can be introduced when:

> printing with one surface of a three-dimensional shape;
> taking rubbings of flat surfaces;
> looking at shadows projected on a screen by shining light on an object;
> making shadows and shadow puppets;
> drawing around objects onto paper;
> opening out boxes of various shapes;
> looking at photographs and pictures;
> looking at reflections in the mirror.

The teacher can talk with the children about the shapes that they see. They may experiment with a variety of shapes.

What shape do they expect to find when they take a rubbing of one surface of a cuboid?

Vocabulary: flat – different – surface – shape – square – triangle – circle – round – rectangle.

Covering surfaces

Experience may be gained by the following activities:

> junk modelling: painting surfaces, covering surfaces with paper; wrapping parcels;
> putting pillow slips on pillows, making beds;
> making paper hats and head-dresses;
> putting tablecloth on table (it doesn't fit exactly, but it covers the surface); or use newspaper;
> "painting" surface of outside wall with a brush and water;
> wallpapering Home Corner or doll's house;
> making carpets, covers for tables and beds, and curtains for doll's house;
> covering surface within cut-out or drawn shape by painting, colouring or spreading plasticine;

> printing a variety of shapes onto a variety of shaped paper;
> tesselations (see Part 1, *Introducing EME*);
> doing jigsaw puzzles;
> making mosaic pictures;
> making a simple "flannelgraph" with felt shapes.

The teacher may encourage children to estimate the size or amount of material, e.g. paper, needed to cover a surface. She can provide a choice of size and shape.

The children can experiment with a variety of shapes and sizes in all the activities listed above.

Any difficulties may be discussed, but the children should be encouraged to solve problems for themselves.

Vocabulary: cover – fits – edge to edge – space – too much – too small – too big – big enough – all – different – straight – curved.

Matching shapes in two dimensions

Some opportunities to match shapes occur in the following activities:

> using cut-out shapes, making comparisons;
> comparing shapes and pictures drawn or printed on cards;
> playing dominoes and snap;
> playing shape matching card games;
> playing "find one that looks like this" (teacher hides similar card or shape nearby);
> copying patterns or shapes, either by painting, drawing or using combinations of cut-out shapes.

The children can look for shapes in pictures and books, and in patterns on material, clothes, street signs, advertisements.

Vocabulary: looks like – sides – edge – point – corner – angle – next to – different – rounded – curved – straight.

Area

Early ideas of invariance and measurement of area may be beginning to develop at this stage. Very young children are confused by the idea of invariance, but as they mature they may develop an interest in it.

The belief that there is "more room" when tables are pushed to one side demonstrates this kind of thinking, in which the perception of a single large area of space rather than many smaller areas, dominates any judgement. The teacher may sometimes ask children when they are playing with doll's house furniture, whether there is more space on the floor when the furniture is pushed to one side, or perhaps may ask them to make a comparison between two similar sized tables with similar toys differently placed.

Vocabulary: more – less – space/room – same – together – apart.

Symmetry

Ideas of symmetry might be developed through experience of folding, pattern making and play with mirrors. Regular shapes (squares, rectangles, circles) can be folded along axes of symmetry, perhaps using everyday objects (handkerchiefs, scarfs). Paper or card might be used and patterns made around the axis fold, or folded after one side of the axis has been painted in some way, to produce the familiar "ink blot" type of picture.

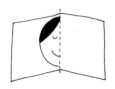 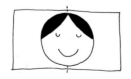

Mirrors can be a good source of fun in relation to the topic of symmetry. They can be used with patterns or incomplete drawings, and there are some books specially produced for this purpose. (Non-breakable "flexible mirrors" are obtainable from Osmiroid Educational Publishers; Mirror books by Marion Walter are published by Andre Deutsch, London.)

Other activities which can involve symmetry include:

> printing, collage, painting patterns on paper with axis of symmetry previously marked;
> looking at and discussing "symmetrical things", e.g. balance, butterfly;
> folding paper in half to cut out symmetrical doll or other shape.

Vocabulary: half – side – back to front.

Perspective

When children sit round the edge of the table to play a game such as "Snap" or do a puzzle, then the view of the cards or pieces is not straightforward and it is more difficult to match. As we and the things about us move, our view of them is constantly changing. A car, for instance, might have a quite different shape when viewed from behind and at the side. This is true of many things; it is true of ourselves. Look at cars going past, planes in the sky, trains and buses, washing frames spinning round, spirals, tops, mobiles. All present us with a different view of them as they move. A rotating wheel or board might encourage talk with the children about the shape of objects rotating on it, whether they are regular geometric, three-dimensional shapes or everyday objects.

Do things look different when the children are standing on chairs or tables? What about those children who live in blocks of flats—do things look different from their windows? Children may enjoy talking about things they have seen and making comparisons from different viewpoints.

Example

Simon (4.6): I've made an elephant. His tail is at the back and his trunk is at the front. You can't see his legs because they are under him. You're looking at him from an aeroplane.

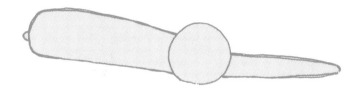

The teacher might initiate other explorations. What about recognising things that are "upside down"? Do things have a "right way up"? What about cups, bottles, jugs, cups and saucers, shoes, pictures? Try putting a picture or book upside down—does anyone notice? Try to guess what is the right way up. Try to estimate the size of things at a distance and check the estimate with the object itself.

Ask the children to move around an object or move the object while the children remain still. When the child is moving, or when the object is moving, the child's view of it changes.

Offer objects held at unusual angles. "What's this?" Discuss pictures of familiar objects seen from different angles.

What do things look like when we're upside down? Identify pictures held "upside down".

Rotate regular geometrical shapes. Do children recognise a triangle when it is not standing on one of its sides, or a square suspended by one corner?

Use transparent perspex to observe the underneath of things like snails or slugs.
What would this look like from a worm's-eye/giant's-eye-view?

Vocabulary: upside down – right way up – low – high – up – down – smaller – larger – edge – rounded – flat – curved – looks like – looks the same – looks different – underneath – side – on top of – at the side – behind – in front of – top – bottom.

Identifying shapes

Experiences like those which have been described in the previous sections will gradually enable each child to develop ideas about shapes. Provision of a range of experience and a willingness to talk with the child about properties and qualities of objects, whether regular or irregular shapes, will offer a basis from which he will later generalise concepts of shape and space.

Many two- and three-dimensional shapes have particular names and it might be helpful to use the correct terms with the children. Emma is quite confident and used to naming shapes.

Example

Emma (4.3) is choosing painting paper and talking to herself. "I think I'll have a square one—no, a triangle."

By encouraging children to use descriptive vocabulary to make comparisons and estimations, and to take part in activities such as sorting and matching, the teacher helps to provide a broad foundation for their later learning.

The teacher's role

Once again it is impossible to emphasise sufficiently our role in talking with children about these and other activities. Obviously there are moments when one would not intrude, but at other times the presence of someone who is interested and willing to talk with the child about his experience will perhaps not only extend his enjoyment and satisfaction but also his thinking.

The teacher provides the materials to be explored. Her awareness can spark the child's interest, encourage investigation and help him to describe what happens. Often the teacher is needed to introduce language to describe movement and position, not just of objects, but of the child himself.

The teacher learns much about the stage of each child's thinking simply by observation.

In this first example, the teacher is content to listen to the group of children who are competently coping with the task in hand.

Example 1
Children were sticking pieces of broken polystyrene tiles on to boxes to make "ice".

Rhona (4.4):	I'm looking for a piece the right size for this hole.
Kate (3.7):	It's like doing a jigsaw.
Rhona:	No, it's not. Jigsaws fit exactly.
Michael (4.1):	This piece is too big to fit in here. (Snaps

some off.) It's still too big. (Snaps more off.) That's just right.

In example 2, Irene knows how to compare the size of two shapes, but is not prepared to make the visual assessment that Andrew does, before she checks.

Example 2
There were several triangular sheets of paper on the table. The teacher asked if they were the same size. Irene (4.0) picked one up and placed it on top of another saying, "Let me see". Andrew (4.4) who had been watching said, "No."

In the next example, Matthew shows that although he recognises the rotated triangle as such, his concept of "triangle" is still dominated by the idea that a triangle "is really stood on a base".

Example 3
A small group was making pictures and patterns using sticky paper shapes. Matthew (4.7) picked up a triangular piece of paper, held it up on one vertex, ∇, looked at it for a moment, then said "It's a triangle, isn't it? But it's upside-down."

The examples which follow show how in each case the teacher's interest and guidance has encouraged the children to talk with her, to share ideas and to try to find their own solutions to any practical problems that they encounter.

Example 4

Jeremy (4.10) was putting away drawers full of toys. The drawer of cars would not fit in.

Jeremy:　These won't go in.

Teacher:　Why do you think that is?

Jeremy:　They are all in a jumble on top of each other.

Teacher:　Do you know what to do to make them fit properly?

Jeremy:　Yes. I'll flatten 'em all tidy.

Example 5

Gary (5.0) and Jason (4.7) were carrying the garage in from the garden and were unable to manoeuvre it through the doorway.

Gary:　We can't get it in. Jason, stop pushing. It won't go.

Teacher:　I think you'll have to turn it round.

Gary:　Come on, Jason. You go *that* way. No, round that way. Come on, that's right.

Having manoeuvered with one boy going through the door backwards, one forwards, the garage came through safely.

Example 6

In the middle of story-time, two helicopters passed over, making, of course, their own distinctive noise. The story was temporarily abandoned while the children crowded to the window to watch the helicopters.

Jacqueline (5.1):　There's one!

Alex (4.7):　No, there's two!

Jacqueline:　I can see the other one now.

General excitement and comments from several children.

Steven (4.4):　They're only little ones.

Joanne (4.10):　Only little ones.

Alex:　They're not really little. It's 'cos they are a long way away.

Gary (5.0):　You mean they are ever so high up.

Victoria (4.8):　They're getting smaller, look.

Jacqueline:　That's 'cos they're going over the river.

Jason (4.8):　I can still see them. They're going over the river.

Alex:　They've gone now.

Example 7

Alex (4.7):　I was at school first!

Teacher:　Yes, I know you were. I had to wait at the traffic lights for a long time.

Alex:　We didn't have to wait 'cos we walked. I saw your car and it was a long way away. It was coming through the [school] gate. It looked very little but it isn't really, is it?

Teacher:　Why do you think it looked so small when you first saw it?

Alex:　I expect it's 'cos you were a long way away. (He looked towards the school gate and saw a bus pass along the main road) Even buses look small, don't they?

Example 8

Jeremy (4.10) threw a ball over the fence, so that it landed in the neighbouring school playing field. The teacher took him to retrieve the ball.

Jeremy:　It's big out here. I wish our garden was all out here, then we'd have lots more room.

Teacher:　It would be good for playing football and having long races, wouldn't it?

Jeremy:　And you could chase me and I could run ever so fast.

Teacher:　There's the ball. Can you see it?

Jeremy:　I can throw it back from here. I can throw a long way. Look!

When he arrived back in the garden, he told the boys playing ball "I threw it back from right over there."

2 Comparisons

Introduction

Exploration of the world about us inevitably leads to comparisons. My hair is *longer than* yours; this pram is *bigger than* that one; my plank is *heavier than* yours; and so on. This chapter will be concerned with such comparisons of just two things (my hair and yours, etc.); children will also compare whole rows of objects (e.g. sticks) and grade them according to size, but this is referred to in another section as "ordering". (See chapters 7 and 8 *Towards Number* and *Apparatus, Toys and Games.*)

Comparison involves an awareness of similarities and differences. The differences may not be visual: there can be differences of texture, weight, odour, taste and temperature. Therefore it is essential that children have as many experiences as possible before and while they are asked to make comparisons. Very young children seem to use a combination of senses when they explore new or familiar objects and although as they grow older most children reject tasting and sucking, the sense of touch accompanies visual discrimination for a long time.

The range of relationships which deal with comparisons is enormous (is *shorter than*; is *fatter than*; is *darker than*; is *colder than*; is *lower than*; and so on). Children begin by making statements like "this one is big", "this one is small", and only later use the comparative form "this one is *bigger than* that one". They may ask for a "big" piece of cake, meaning one that is thick, long or wide, and, comparing their dinners, will say that the dinner which covers more of the plate is the bigger one, without comparing the actual quantity.

Example
John (3.9):   I've had an enormous dinner.
Andrew (3.8):   I've had a bigger dinner than you. Mine was as big as the moon.

"As big as the moon."

In fact, most young children use the words "big" and "little" indiscriminately, and while it is most important not to make them feel wrong for doing so, they can be encouraged to use the appropriate words by hearing them from their teachers.

With help, a child can progress from talking about a "big tree" to describing a "tall" one. Then trying to express himself more clearly, it becomes "a tree that is taller than the one in the garden". Thus he has established a relationship between the tree he is talking about and another one known also to the listener.

This leads on to making different kinds of relationships, including that of *is greater than*, when establishing an order in any set of numbers. Relations and sets are dealt with more fully in Part II of *Mathematics—the First Three Years.* (Nuffield Mathematics Project and C.E.D.O., W. & R. Chambers and John Murray, 1970.)

Possible developments

Length, height, width, depth

a) When playing with bricks, children often call adults to admire their work, thus opening the way for questions.

> You have built a tall tower. Can you see some other things that are as tall?
> That's a long road you have built. How much longer can you make it? How can you make it wide enough to push the pram along?
> Do you think that John's tower is taller than yours? (If the towers are not near enough to see which is the taller, suggest that they cut a strip of paper or string to match one tower and then compare this strip with other towers.)

Questions like these will help a child to answer with more than just "yes" or "no" and the conversations which follow may produce even more mathematical ideas.

b) Constructional toys are often compared. When children are playing together, one invariably claims to have built the biggest model. Whilst agreeing that one is taller, longer or wider we can also say that the other one is lower, shorter or narrower. There is always a reverse expression (if my boat is *heavier than* yours, then your boat is *lighter than* mine) and every opportunity should be taken to give children experiences which will help to develop this. Comments might include, "Is your robot as tall as the table? Can you make a taller one?"

c) Climbing bars and frames give plenty of experience in getting higher and lower, although young children find these experiences difficult to put into words and they are not always sure about the distinction, for example, between "higher" and "taller", when making comparisons between people or objects on different levels.

Example
Some children made a robot, which was about 1.5 m tall, from junk materials. Each child stood against the robot and they found that they were all shorter than it. When the teacher stood against it she was found to be taller. But when the robot was standing on a workbench it appeared to be taller than the teacher and the children, in fact, thought it had become taller in some way.

d) Children soon begin to compare their own heights: "I can reach up to that shelf but Johnny can reach up to the top shelf". Careful use of words will ensure that "taller" is only used when comparing two objects or people that are standing on the same level. When one is raised in some way, e.g. on a box, table, cupboard, climbing frame or staircase, it becomes "higher" than the other, but not "taller" unless it was taller to start with.

e) Long mirrors can be helpful: if two children stand together they can see which is taller or shorter. A child and an adult can be compared: the child can then stand on a box or brick and become higher but not taller.

f) Furniture, toys or chairs sometimes need to be moved

from room to room. Is it wider than the doorway? Is it taller/higher than the door?

Example
Louise (4.6) invited her teacher to tea in the playhouse. "You can sit here", she said, pointing to a small chair with arms. As teacher was about to sit down, Louise said, "You can't sit there, you're too big. Sit on the stool." Louise was able to compare size when she saw the problem. With further conversation, she might say "You are too wide for the chair", or "The chair is too narrow for you".

g) Very large bricks, hidey-hole boxes, planks and steps involve many comparisons and children often call adults to join their play. Questions can be asked such as:

> Can you make a bridge with this plank so that I can reach you? Is it long enough? Is the doorway wide enough for the doll's pram?
> Can you stand up inside your house? Is it high enough? Can I get through the doorway?

Given this last problem, some children will make a second larger doorway while keeping the first smaller one for its original purpose.

h) Some schools are lucky enough to have landscaped gardens with hillocks and tunnels where there are many experiences of comparison:

> Are you higher than the sand pit when you are on top of the hill? What can you see over the top of the school when you are on the hill? Can you see who is lower down the hill than you?

i) The sand pit, paddling pool, holes in the ground and ditches can all give experience of depth:

> The water comes up to your knees, but over the top

of Mary's knees. When you go down the steps, the water gets higher and higher up your legs.
> Can you dig a hole in the sand deeper than mine?
> In the garden, a daffodil bulb needs a deep hole, but the marigold seeds only need a shallow hole.

By talking and interacting with children we can gradually increase their understanding of the various terms used to describe length, height, depth and width and they will come to differentiate between them.

Vocabulary: higher – lower – taller – shorter – longer – wider – narrower – thinner – thicker – deeper – shallower – as high as – as long as – as wide as – high enough – long enough – wide enough – too high – too long – too wide.

Area

At this age children find it difficult to estimate area and would not be expected to use the term. Nevertheless there are some activities that will provide the opportunity to ask the children to compare different areas.

> Which tablecloth shall we use to cover the tea-table? If it is too big, the edges will touch the floor. If it is too small, it will not cover the table.
> Will your junk model fit on to that shelf? Is there enough room?
> Can we all sit on this blue mat? Will we be less squashed on the red one?

This type of question may only receive one-word answers, but the response will show the stage of awareness that a child has reached. More stimulation and experiences can then be offered in some of the following ways:

a) Show a child some circles of paper or material and ask him to take as many as he thinks he would need to cover a certain piece of paper. Then by sticking them on he can find out if he needs more or less. This can be repeated with smaller or larger circles, or commercially produced shapes. There can be no right or wrong answer as "covering" may mean overlapping, leaving symmetrical spaces or a perfect tesselation, but it may lead to comparison of results between child, teacher and other children.

b) Directed and spontaneous craft activities provide some of the best opportunities for comparisons:

> Do we need more coloured paper to cover this Corn Flakes box than this chocolate box?
> Which piece of paper is the right size to cover the front/back/side/underneath of this box?

c) Outdoor activities can also provide opportunities for comparison. "More children can fit into this circle painted on the ground than into the smaller one." We need more children to stand round this tree joining hands than round that tree."

Vocabulary: more . . . than – less . . . than – close together – far apart – fit – same as – too many – not enough.

Weight

a) Many objects which look alike are in fact of different weight, and children love to "try the difference". There are so many obvious examples. A few are given here. Compare, first by looking, then by holding:

> a golf ball and a table tennis ball;
> a hollow wooden brick and a solid wooden brick;
> an empty bottle and one full of water;

Remember to ask the question both ways. Which one is lighter? Which one is heavier?

b) Let children feel the objects in their hands before they begin to use even the simplest balance (e.g. coathanger). Then they can discover that the object that felt heavier in their hands is the one that goes down bang on one side of the balance. Let them help find similar pairs of boxes, tins, etc., fill one of each pair with sand (dry or wet), or pebbles, then seal and wrap them to look alike. They can "feel the difference" between parcels that look alike and try them on the balance. A great deal of practical experience is necessary here before children begin to generalise and know that the heavier article will always go down, although it may look smaller. This will lead to much experiment and comparisons between, for example, an air-filled balloon and a small plastic brick.

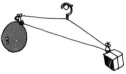

c) Children like to compare their own weight on such things as seesaws. The heavier child may question why he goes down bump.

d) Push and pull toys give experience of the weight of more than one child. Taking a pram or tricycle up a slope or shallow steps will often lead a child to say "This is too heavy for me. I need another boy to help."

Vocabulary: heavier – lighter – balance – full – empty – hollow – solid – too much – not enough – too heavy.

Volume and mass

Example

Samantha (4.9):	The apple is smaller than mine now.
Teacher:	Why?
Samantha:	Because she has eaten some of it.

Very young children quickly learn to recognise "more", e.g. more dinner, more milk, but "less" takes longer to understand. It is intangible, not there to be seen or felt, and can only be gauged by imagining what might have been. In conversation with children we can take every opportunity to introduce these words into their vocabulary so that they begin to understand there is more than one way that comparisons can be expressed.

a) When we make comparisons of volume we are trying to find which container holds more or less than another.

Example
Christopher (4.0) and Wayne (4.0), playing at the water tray, discussed the containers they were filling with water. "Let me have your jug. It holds more water than mine and I want to fill this big teapot."

There are many activities in the sand and water tray leading children to compare.

> Is this castle larger than that one?
> Will the sand from that castle fit into this bucket?
> Will this bucket fit over this castle?
> Which bucket holds more sand? Which holds less?

With bottles of different sizes comparisons of volume can be made.

> Can you pour all the water from that bottle into this bottle? Is there a space? Do you need more water to fill it up? Which bottle holds less? Which bottle holds more?

b) One time that children frequently make comparisons is when they are drinking their milk.

Example
Vanessa (4.5):   I've got more than you.
Victoria (5.4):   If you drink some, we will have the same.
They compared heights of milk in their bottles.

Sometimes children use mugs for their milk and a large bottle may be shared between several mugs. Watching the level of the milk go down in the bottle, a child may query that there will be enough left for the last person. He can then be encouraged to look at the mugs and, if they are all of similar size and shape, he can compare the level to see if there is more or less in any. A more mature child may even be led to experiment with different shapes of mugs and compare the height of a liquid in a tall, thin mug with the same liquid poured into a short fat one. Piaget (Piaget, Jean. *The Child's Conception of Number*, Chapter I, Routledge & Kegan Paul, 1952) has written about many experiments conducted with children from the age of four, and found that they did not understand this concept of invariance until much later.

Example
Kerry (4.3) is showing us a clear example of this lack of understanding when she says, "Our bottle of milk won't fit into the rabbit's dish. It will *fall over the top*."

c) When using clay, dough or plasticine, children often ask for more when they are modelling an animal or figure. Try sharing a large piece of dough between two children as equally as possible. Leave them to model and then suggest that they compare their models. If they are similar, e.g. pots, snakes or pancakes, the sizes can be compared and discussion may arise concerning thickness or length. If different, e.g. a hollow cup and a solid ball, we can ask if they still both have the same amount of clay. Again, this idea of the invariance of mass will not be fully understood until a much later stage.

d) Bricks and boxes need to be packed away. If we pack them tidily into a corner or under a shelf, for example, will they take up less space than if we leave them in an untidy heap? There are many opportunities, when "clearing up", to compare the amount of space needed for the junk boxes, balls, musical instruments and toys.

Many more new words will occur as these activities are explored with the children, but it will be some time before they understand the abstract expressions "more than" and "less than". "More clay than", "more pudding than" have much more meaning for a young child. At the same time, children are inventing their own expressions and reasons, as in the following example.

Example

Teacher: (Handing a large piece of crumpled paper to Darren.) Will you put this in the waste bin?

Darren (4.2): No, it's too big.

Darren could see that the open sheet of paper would not fit into the bin. More activities and experiences of the kind described in Chapter 1, *Space and Shape*, would help him to understand the ways that the shape of materials may be changed.

Vocabulary: thicker – fatter – thinner – smaller – larger – full – empty – level – too much – too little – more – more than – less – less than.

Double comparisons

Very young children are generally unable to concentrate on more than one detail at a time. It would therefore be unnecessarily confusing to deliberately ask them to make "double" comparisons. On the other hand, there are occasions when this arises spontaneously.

a) Sorting through pieces of material for a collage picture, we might well say, "Yes, that's the right colour but it's too thick" thus helping the child to become more selective without rejecting his first choice completely. Waste materials of all sorts are often used for sorting and collage work. Boxes can be compared. One may be shorter and deeper than another or longer and thinner.

b) Trying to put a funnel on a junk box boat, a child may reject an empty custard tin in favour of a tube from a paper towel roll. "The tin is *shorter* and *wider* than the roll."

c) Trees in a group may look alike from a distance, but on closer inspection, some look tall and narrow, others shorter and wider-spreading.

d) Children playing with bricks of varying sizes will sometimes refer to the "strongest" one where they cannot make a comparison of length, height and width all at once. Whilst playing with them it may be possible to extend their vocabulary in this direction.

e) Attribute blocks and similar apparatus can be used for comparison. While these are usually offered as a free choice toy, some of the more mature children begin to sort them by more than one attribute and then we can join their play and suggest other games.

Sort the red and thin.   Sort the thick and blue.
Sort the thin and square.   Sort the blue and triangular.

Probably the best way to start is to ask the child to tell the teacher two attributes of a certain piece. If he volunteers that it is square and thin, it can be assumed that he recognises these attributes and can find other pieces that will match.

Distance and magnification

As young children's eyes begin to focus correctly, they recognise objects at a greater distance, but do not understand perspective. An aeroplane can only be judged for size if they have had experience of the object close at hand. Experience tells us that the single seater biplane is smaller than the jet air liner, although being at different altitudes they appear to be the same size. Young children explore the problem by questioning adults. They might get the reply "It looks small because it's a long way away." Michael (3.0), watching an aeroplane fly over, "It's a big aeroplane". Fiona (4.0) "When it comes down it's big." Sven (4.8) shows his level of understanding, "When you get nearer and nearer you get big and when you get farer and farer (*sic*) you get small."

Some activities involving the concept of distance are:

a) Look at two footballs, then take one to the further end of the garden or playground. Come back to the door and then ask, Can you still see it? How big does it look? Does it look smaller than the one we have here?

b) Make some paper kites or blow up some balloons. Let them go high into the sky on a windy day and see if they look smaller than before.

Children love to use magnifying glasses. There are many varieties—small hand-held lenses, large tripod mounted glasses, lenses on the end of flexible stands, and sets of clear plastic jars with screw-on magnifying lids. The latter are especially useful as they can contain pebbles, shells, pieces of cotton, flowers, seeds, etc. Children can look at the contents with and without the lid, and like to see the contents appearing to "get bigger".

Donna (4.9) was looking through a magnifying glass.

"The cress is big. It's not really big, it's small, but it's growing bigger, then it will look as high as the ceiling."

Vocabulary: near – far – further – nearer – near to – far away from – bigger – smaller.

Number

As soon as comparisons are made by number instead of quantity the expression becomes "how many" and not "how much". Although very young children may be able to recite numbers in their correct sequence, they do not appreciate that twenty is more than fifteen, for example. There are a number of activities that will lead them to compare numbers of separate items by one-to-one matching, without actually counting them.

a) Are there more boys here today than girls? Make a line of boys and match a girl to each. Are there some girls left over? If so, there must be more girls than boys.

b) Are there as many brushes as there are pots of paint? Put one brush in each pot; are there any over? If not, there are as many brushes as pots.

c) Compare a box of shells with a box of beads. Put the shells in a line and match a bead to each one. Are there more shells than beads? How many more shells than beads? This will be a smaller number to count than the total number of either shells or beads and the answer will have more meaning than saying there are seventeen shells and fifteen beads.

d) Threading beads always leads to comparison and if the beads are of similar size and shape, it is easy to see that there are two more white than black.

Vocabulary: more than – less than – as many as – share – one each – left over.

The teacher's role

In all these activities, making comparisons of length, area, mass, volume, weight and number, the active interest of an adult is essential. It is by hearing both new and familiar words that children learn to express their thoughts more clearly, and make their judgements more accurately. Rather than attempting formal lessons on "comparisons", it is more profitable to avail oneself of the opportunities arising from the children's play and the everyday running of the group. The following example, wherein the teacher leaves the children to work out the problem, but is still involved, shows this in a simple straightforward way.

Example 1

Some new furniture was delivered and difficulty was experienced in trying to move some of the tables into the classroom.

Nigel (4.11):   Alan and me will carry this table.
Alan (4.10):   We have to change it round; it's too wide to get through the door.
Teacher: What about the round table?
Nigel: Oh, we'll never get it out. We'll have to smash the windows.
Teacher: I don't think I'd like that.
Nigel: Well, we can't get that table out. It will get stuck.
Michael (4.9):   We can turn it on its side, then the door will be wide enough.
Nigel: No, we'll have to cut the legs off now.
Michael: No, we'll be able to get it through.

Nigel: I don't believe it.
Teacher: Well, let's see if it will go through.
Nigel: It has gone right through. It fits exactly!

Again, in the following incident the teacher supplies just enough information to lead the child on.

Example 2

Alan (4.10) found some old weights and was playing with them.

Alan: Look, I've got one of these.
Teacher: Is it heavy?
Alan: Yes, it's very heavy.
Teacher: That is a weight. We use it on scales.
Alan: Here's another one.
Teacher: Which one is heavier?
Alan: They are both the same heavy.

It is important that children are not interrupted in such a way as to destroy their own ideas and pleasure in order to make a mathematical point, but the next example shows that sometimes there is a right way and time to make a suggestion.

Example 3

Some four-year-olds were baking jam tarts.

Ian (4.6):   I have more than you.
Stuart (4.4):   You've just rolled yours more.
Glen (4.3):   But Ian can make more tarts so he must have more.

The children were told to roll the pastry into balls again and agreed that the three balls were all the same size.

Teacher: If they are the same, how could Ian make three tarts and you could only make two?

Glen: Ian spread his thinner.

Moving furniture and effects into a newly decorated room gave the class in the following example many chances to make comparisons, as the teacher and children worked together.

Example 4

Mavis (5.1): Can I carry that box?

Teacher: Sorry, Mavis, it's far too heavy. You can take that one.

Mavis: But that one's heavier.

Teacher: No, it isn't, it's lighter. It's just got frieze paper in it.

Mavis: But it's bigger than that one.

Teacher: Maybe, but that one has jigsaws and games in it and they're heavier.

Mavis: Let me try. Oh! The big one is lighter. I can carry it. I'm strong.

Roy (4.11): I'll take this one. (Indicating a box the same size as Mavis was now carrying.)

Teacher: You can't lift that one, Roy, it's too heavy for you.

Roy: But Mavis is carrying that one.

Teacher: Yes, but it has frieze paper in it. That one has books.

Roy: Phew! It is heavy. I can't even push it. Can I carry them [the books] one at a time?

When children come to show something they have made, the remark need not always be "Oh, that's lovely!" An open-ended question or remark gives the child a chance to think about what he has done.

Example 5

Teacher: What have you made out of poppets?

Maureen (4.6): A necklace.

Teacher: Is it for you?

Maureen: No, it's for my baby.

Teacher: Why is it not for you?

Maureen: It isn't a big enough hole.

The next incident shows how a teacher responded to a simple question, leading the children forward, reinforcing previous experiences and introducing new vocabulary.

Example 6

Andrew (4.9): What are those knobs on your chair for?

Teacher: To adjust the height of the chair. Shall I show you what we can do?

Matt (3.11): The chair is very big now.

Teacher: Was the seat as high as this before?

Paul (4.9): It's higher now.

Andrew: It's grown taller. Before it was small.

Teacher: Shall we make it shorter again?

Matt: Now it's little.

Paul: It is shorter and smaller.

Andrew: Flats are bigger.

Teacher: Bigger than what, Andrew?

Paul: Bigger and higher than houses.

Teacher: Can you think of something smaller than a house?

Paul: A cottage, and some flats.

Teacher: What sort of flats do you mean, Paul?

Paul: Little flats where you can't go upstairs.

Teacher: That's right, Paul. You mean where some old people live in bungalows near you.

These actual examples show teachers observing children, extending and reinforcing ideas they have already assimilated, and ready to offer the next step forward in the children's mathematical thinking.

3 Home Corner

Introduction

The importance of Home Corner play for young children has long been accepted. Many schools have, where possible, extended the provision to include more than one all-purpose Home Corner room, and sometimes children have a "kitchen", "lounge" and "bedroom" in which to play.

Other areas such as the shop, supermarket or hairdressers are often set up and, if not permanently established like the Home Corner, are used and replaced, to return again months later and be enjoyed with renewed enthusiasm.

Opportunity for mathematical experience and the development of mathematical thinking might seem unlikely to occur readily in the Home Corner. Unlikely, that is, until we consider the range of equipment and materials that children handle as they play. A child's use of the equipment may well reflect previous learning; it may be imitative or imaginative, but will certainly provide first hand experience of using and organising everyday objects, together with opportunities for experiment with the way they behave.

Example
In the Home Corner, Andrew (4.5) is trying to put the largest pan into the oven.
Andrew: It's going to be rice and I can't put it in.
Teacher: Will it fit on the top shelf?
Andrew: I'll take the lid off, then it will go in.

Simply by providing a variety of equipment and allowing the children to experiment, we are effectively increasing the possibility for incidental mathematical experience and learning.

Example
Phillip (4.7):   Just look at those pans. Someone's put all the wrong lids on.
He then replaced the three lids correctly according to size.

The concern for order that Phillip shows is perhaps unusual in young children, who share little of the attention to detail or sequence needed for complicated adult existence.

Example
Ann (4.4) was asked to tidy the prams at the end of the day, i.e. give each pram one pillow, one sheet, one blanket, one doll. The sheets, etc. were put on the table with the dolls, and an explanation given. Ann nodded, yes, she could, and was left by herself to do it. She put all the dolls in one pram and covered them with four sheets and four blankets.

Concern for ideas like one-to-one correspondence is often of minimal importance in the child's imaginative play, when the need may be primarily emotional or social. At other times, however, when play seems to be faltering, a visit by a genuinely interested adult might be acceptable and suggestions appropriate.

I'm hungry! Let's lay the table for tea.
Is there one cup each?
Your baby's crying, she's so cold. Why don't you dress her?
My goodness, this house is untidy. Let's have a spring clean.

It may not work out that way, but the teacher here has, of course, had matching, ordering and sorting in mind.

The child's play often reflects experience in school and at home. Many children will not be used to "sit down meals" or "laying the table", for instance, and skills like these may be learned in purposeful activities in school and practised spontaneously in play.

"Four for tea"

Example

Helen (4.4):   We need another knife—I've only got two and I need three.

She found a knife in the cutlery drawer and set three places with cups, saucers, plates, knives, forks and spoons.

Tidying away can, of course, involve ideas of space and shape, one-to-one correspondence, sorting and ordering. The provision of suitable storage space within each area, so that most things have a place in which they fit or belong, enables children to try to tidy up for themselves, though they will doubtless need their teacher's help to begin with.

The play taking place in the Home Corner might at times be imaginative, and at other times imitative. In his imaginative play, the child in part creates a world of his own and the creatures or objects in it. In imitative play he might assume a role in imitation of one with which he is familiar and might handle equipment as he has seen it used by others.

There are inevitably occasions when an interested and sensitive adult may very well be welcomed into the child's imaginative play, and a "visitor" in the role of house guest, window cleaner or plumber, may even serve to extend the play by providing extra stimuli and ideas. On the other hand, the arrival of an adult "observer" or "intruder" may shatter the illusion and bring the play to a halt.

Certainly, the arrival of an uninvited and unwelcome mathematically obsessed visitor would hardly be inclined to keep anyone at home!

Possible developments

Home Corner—equipment

Much of the mathematical experience in the Home Corner will be an integral and incidental part of the child's free play with the equipment provided. There is a need for good quality equipment, and by varying the colour, shape and size of things provided, the opportunity may be extended for one-to-one correspondence, sorting and ordering. These are experiences which lead towards number and are explained more fully in chapters 7 and 8, *Towards Number* and *Apparatus, Toys and Games*. Differences are likely to stimulate choice; the smallest chair might be most suitable for the "baby", place settings might each be of a different colour, saucepans might be chosen by size to fit the ring available.

Example
Alexandra (4.3) quite spontaneously sorted a set of pots, matched each with the right-sized lid and graded them on a shelf by size.

Below is a list of equipment which is available for use in Home Corner areas, though quite obviously any one Home Corner will contain only a selection of the items mentioned. The provision of the equipment does not ensure the mathematical experience, but can create opportunity for it. Possible mathematical experiences are given for activities involving each item.

Screen: Arranging furniture inside, altering shape of usable floor space. Is there enough "room"?
Moving furniture, selves or prams through door.

Cooker: Might notice shapes of "electric rings", doors, knobs, etc.

Sink unit: (Bowl and soapy water.) Fitting "washing up" into bowl, perhaps displacing water.

Dresser: Fitting cups, saucers, plates, tins, etc. into cupboards or onto shelves.

Curtains: Children perhaps deciding shape and size.
Covering surface when pulled across window; apparently changing shape when pushed back.
Patterns in curtain material.

Carpet: Covering surface.
Fitting into available space.
Using edge of carpet as boundary, arranging furniture within or outside boundary.
Pattern in carpet design.

Carpet tiles: Rearranging and combining in different patterns and shapes.

Table cloth: Covering surface.
Sometimes the design in the centre of cloth might be used to place it centrally.
Folding.

Cruet set: Fitting pieces onto tray.
Set of three.

Tray: Fitting objects onto tray.
Carrying empty/full tray.

Ironing board and iron: Folding to put away, unfolding to use.
Ironing surfaces.

Clothes basket: Filling and emptying basket; fitting "washing" into basket.

Chest of drawers: Filling/emptying drawers.
Folding, altering shapes to fit.
Fitting drawers into appropriate spaces.

Dish cloth/mop: Cleaning surfaces of plates.
Wiping surfaces of tables, draining board.
Reaching inside bottles etc. to clean them.

Plate rack: Fitting crockery, etc. into rack.

Mirror: Reflections.
(Sometimes promotes talk if placed near telephone—children "talk to" mirror.)

Knives, forks, spoons: Sorting.

Cutlery tray: Sorting.

"Food": (All kinds) Variety of imitation foods and sweets might be sorted and shared.

Fruit (imitation) and bowl: Sets of different varieties, colours, etc.

Flowers and vases: Arranging flowers in vases.

Cot/covers/doll: Fitting dolls into right beds, covering them with blankets.

Table and chairs: Matching chairs to people or dolls.
Fitting chairs around table.

Cups, saucers, plates: Matching cup to saucer.
Matching sets of cups, saucers, plates or place settings.

Saucepans: (graded sizes) Matching lids to saucepans, saucepan to "hot plate".
Finding lids that fit.

Place mats: Giving one each.
Perhaps paint place setting onto mats so that knives and forks can be matched to picture.

Clothes rail or rack: Hanging clothes on hangers.
Hanging clothes next to each other along rail.
Putting shoes on racks.

Dolls and clothes: (Different sizes, colours, etc. perhaps in sets.)
Dressing dolls with clothes that fit.

Clothes line and pegs: Ordering.

Telephone: (Disused real one if possible!)
Perhaps might encourage recognition of number symbols.

Clock: Possible number recognition.
Play with alarm to "time" things.
Move hands of toy clock to appropriate time, e.g. "12" when "lunch-time".

Teapot: Filling and emptying.
Pouring "tea" into cups.

Some other ways in which Home Corner play might be developed

New opportunities are created when play spontaneously extends beyond the Home Corner area. Some of the different ways in which play might develop are outlined below.

Separate rooms
Mention has already been made of the many Home Corners with more than one "room". Where this is not a

permanent possibility, then it is sometimes possible to introduce a temporary partition. This can lead to talk comparing the amount of space and the position of furniture. The furniture can be sorted into the two sections. Some Home Corners have even extended onto split levels or two floors, where raised areas have been used for this purpose.

Vocabulary: more than – less than – smaller than – larger than – inside – outside – around – between – next to – through – on top of – underneath – up – down.

Water

Obviously not all Home Corners are suitable for the use of water for "washing up", "tea" or "washing clothes". Plastic bowls of water are occasionally used in the sink, but more often water activities are set up elsewhere as extensions of the Home Corner play.

Children may use the classroom sink or water tray to wash the cups or the dolls' clothes. In the summer, washday may happen out of doors, and can stimulate lots of talk and

valuable practical experience as children add soap to the water, wash the clothes (taking care that water doesn't flood over the sides of the bowl), wring the clothes and peg them out on a line.

Vocabulary: full – half full – empty – more – less – too much – not enough – upside down – top – bottom – side – next to.

Food

Children are often encouraged to make the "food" for their Home Corner play themselves, usually with flour and water dough that is moulded, hardened and painted. Making the food in this way gives incidental experience of imitating shape and making comparisons, and painting involves covering all the surface area.

Foodstuff varies from fried egg and chips to sausage rolls and sponge cakes. Containers are provided so that, if not during play, then at the close of Home Corner play, there is a simple sorting exercise to be done.

Matching often occurs when food is served, but the sharing may be haphazard. An occasional word from an adult visitor may, if appropriate, direct attention to the problem and its solution. Activity elsewhere, at milk time or after a baking session, might also be of help.

Vocabulary: looks like – more than – fewer than – as many as – one (two) each – all – on top – underneath – inside – together – next to – larger than – smaller than – round – straight – curved.

Moving house

Moving house in real life can be a great worry to young children. Providing opportunity for this to be "played out" in the security of the school can be of help. It can also give plenty of incidental mathematical experiences, posing practical problems of choosing and clearing sufficient space, and of moving and arranging the furniture. Ideas and vocabulary of space, shape and comparisons are likely to be involved. Many schools have furniture which can be used for play outside and children will often supplement this with improvised "furniture" from cardboard boxes, for instance.

Moving house.

Vocabulary: too wide – too long – through – inside – outside – next to – on top of – underneath.

Rhymes and stories

Sometimes stories and rhymes influence children's spontaneous play. (See chapter 12 *Rhymes and Stories*.) Traditional stories, or more recent ones like *Mrs Mopple's Washing Line* or the *Topsy and Tim* series, contain many ideas that children might choose for their Home Corner play.

(Hewett, A. *Mrs Mopple's Washing Line*, Bodley Head, 1966; Adamson, J. and Adamson G. *Topsy and Tim* series, Blackie, 1971.)

Other opportunities

Tea parties—birthday parties in particular.
Dinner time.
Spring cleaning.
Washday.
Picnic—for teddy bears?
Packing for holidays.

The Shop

Not all children will be familiar with shops and shopping. A visit to the local supermarket may well be within their experience, but they may not really have been involved with the shopping itself. A visit in small groups to a local shop might well be a worthwhile preliminary to the introduction of a class shop and may affect the use that the children make of it. (See chapter 10 *The Environment*.)

Very young children often enjoy play with improvised materials. Dried peas, beans or shells stored in durable containers can be much more satisfying than empty packets which, unless regularly replaced, tend to fall apart so easily. Simple balances and a variety of pots and containers can then add variety to the experience of filling, emptying and sharing. Boxes and pots in good condition can, of course, be sorted and arranged on shelves. Tins if originally opened upside down, can be stood the right way up on shelves to look unused, provided that rough and dangerous edges are made quite safe first.

At this stage the act of shopping itself may depend on a very primitive and haphazard rate of exchange, possibly one-to-one. Children are encouraged to play freely and imaginatively, but at a later stage may be helped to give goods a price-marking of counters, e.g. a packet marked with ⠒ would only be exchanged for four counters.

It might be useful to make a simple "stocktaking" book with pictures to match the things in the shop. The older children might then check the "stock" once in a while by one-to-one correspondence.

"Two of those, please."

Again the shop need not be an all-purpose grocers, but might be a supermarket, sweet shop or toy shop, or even a post office with sticky-paper stamps, a letter-box and a postman.

The mathematical ideas which are likely to occur in play in the shop, particularly when children have worked with their teacher to plan and organise it, are those of sorting, matching, ordering, comparisons, shape and space. Each type of shop will offer experience with different kinds of materials.

Vocabulary: all – some – one (two . . .) – empty – full – bigger (taller, wider, longer) than – smaller (shorter, thinner) than – more than – fewer than – less than – inside – outside – next to – on top of.

The café

This area is probably more suited to the older children, and offers opportunity for experience of sorting, matching, comparisons and shape.

With help, the children can prepare "food", lay the tables and serve their customers. Some "cafés" have opted to use a simple pictorial menu, a few use a very simple "price list".

A kitchen set up at a nearby "dough" table can provide the "food"—cakes, biscuits, sausage rolls or sandwiches. A group baking session might provide the real thing, and with careful supervision a real tea might be prepared and served as a special treat.

Vocabulary: more – full – half full – empty – one (two . . .) each – too many – too few – larger than – smaller than – too much – enough.

The hairdressers

Although problems of hygiene do exist, many schools choose to develop the "hairdressers" as an extra play area. Once again, the kind of play and the extent of mathematical experience which it includes will inevitably vary.

The use of rollers of varying size, colour and shape might be spontaneously sorted into trays provided. Safe grips can be used and the appropriate sized roller used for each length of hair; dolls or wigs may be used for this.

Hair nets can be used to cover the dolls' or dummies' heads. Real water for washing dolls' hair provides experience of filling and emptying. Mirrors can stimulate an interest in reflection and prompt children to talk about themselves. Talk and general discussion might include ideas of number, shape and comparisons.

Vocabulary: full – empty – half full – larger than – smaller than – round – spiral – longer than – shorter than – on top of – over.

The hospital corner

The function of the hospital corner is to allow children to play out imaginatively fears and worries resulting from real experience at the hospital or doctor's surgery. Young children may not be aware of the dangers of drugs and medicines, and, of course, it would be dangerous to provide "sweet" imitations.

Beds enable the children themselves to be patients. Bandages of various shapes and sizes can be used and fitted according to the nature of each "injury". Sticking plasters, perhaps made from paper or sticky tape, again in different shapes and sizes, offer choice and comparison. There is, after all, always some status attached to wearing the largest plaster from the real First Aid Kit, even for the smallest scratch! Beds must be made, equipment sorted and ordered, and patients dealt with one at a time.

Mathematical experience can be an integral part of this play, in particular in the child's improvisation of materials which is often quite fascinating.

"Eat it all up. It'll make you better."

Vocabulary: fits – too long – not long enough – too short – wider than – long enough.

The bus

The creation of a bus needs only a collection of chairs and sufficient space for them to be arranged appropriately. This arrangement can be mathematical once the play is under way; a conductor or driver may soon assume responsibility for matching passengers to seats and the children will encounter problems of too many, not enough, empty, etc.

Some children can be encouraged to use improvised tickets, and occasionally "money" can be used in exchange. In some classes the bus is used in conjunction with other areas, so that a group might "take a bus ride" to the "shop" or to "visit friends" in the Home Corner. Used outdoors in the summer the bus might go "to the country" or "the seaside" or off to "a picnic".

Vocabulary: inside – outside – front – back – first, second, etc. – one each – too many – full – empty – next – one (two . . .) more.

The teacher's role

There are many other areas and themes of play which the children might choose to develop that have not been mentioned here. It is important to remember that imaginative/imitative play is a valuable part of the child's early experience. The teacher may initiate ideas through the provision of new and varied equipment and the use of stories or rhymes, but the development of the play arises from the spontaneous interest of the children themselves.

The teacher can learn much about the children's thinking by observing the way that children handle and use the equipment. There are times when she will be included in their play and might decide to develop an opportunity for exploring mathematical ideas which have occurred.

The following examples show how teachers have watched children make use of different materials in spontaneous activity.

In the first example, a chance happening develops into a mathematical experience. Under the watchful eye of the teacher the children improvise their shoe shop, and probably it is she who suggests the use of shelves for the "display" of pairs. Later, she decides to pursue their interest by initiating the tracing and matching activity.

Example 1   The shoe shop
A box of different types of shoes was left near the Home Corner by accident. The children immediately seized on this, and with permission emptied the contents on the floor. Within minutes they had quite voluntarily created a shoe shop.

From this came experience of matching, sorting and comparisons. Talk of size and shape: "Mine's larger and fatter than yours." "Give me that short one to go with this." "This shoe's too small for me, but it might fit you."

The children enjoyed sorting the shoes into pairs. They arranged them on the shelves: "There's too many for this shelf. Put a few over there."

Later, shoe-shapes were traced on black card. The cut-outs were used for matching to the shoes.

The next example is an account of a teacher's observation of children at play whereby she learns of the children's own discoveries as they experiment for themselves.

Example 2   The Supermarket
The children stacked tins as for display in a supermarket. Similar sizes were put together and the piles were symmetrical. Loading shopping baskets to the full, they had experience of capacity. "I want a bigger basket than this. You have mine. You only want a little one for those few tins."

By filling empty tins and jam jars with peas, lentils etc., and also with larger objects like apples and nuts, they discovered for themselves that many small, but few larger, things fill the same container.

The teacher in Example 3 provided a box of dolls' clothes of different sizes and designs. The children are left to find out which ones will fit each doll.

Example 3   Dressing dolls
The box of dolls' clothes is on the table. Susan (4.8) combs the dolls' hair while Cheryl (4.7) sorts out the clothes, measuring the dresses against each doll to see if it's "big enough". Susan insists that none of them are big enough and Cheryl is equally insistent that the right sized one is. There is great hilarity when they find clothes that are obviously "too small".

Cheryl decides, "I'm going to tidy up first". She sorts out the vests trying several against the doll and saying, "It's only half way up her". She then sorts all the vests and folds them up and puts them in the box, then the pants, then dresses and lastly cardigans.

Meanwhile Susan dresses her doll; vest, then pants and dress. Cheryl smiles when she notices a different shade of wool on one sleeve of a cardigan. "It's got two different reds." She measures a too-small all-in-one suit against her doll and laughs, "Look, Sue, look!"

In the last example, the teacher has joined the children as they wash their dolls. It is probably her presence that encourages the children to compare the size of the dolls and to talk about things they notice as they play. The teacher does not allow the "unnatural" pursuit of any mathematical ideas to spoil the children's enjoyment of the activity.

Example 4   Doll washing
Three children are washing dolls. They decide to use warm water. They all rub the soap on the dolls and rub and rub them, then splash up the water till the soap "comes off". They decide the soap makes the water "white".

Julie (4.6):   My doll's legs are longer than Susan's. Susan's got a little doll.
Steven (4.7):   She has got baby's legs.

They decide if you rub the soap on the dolls hard enough with water you "get little bubbles". Julie dropped the soap in the water and Susan (4.8) said, "It will melt". They stand the dolls together and Julie says, "Mine is bigger than hers". They then see how far the water comes up the dolls' legs. They find it takes a lot of water "to rinse off the soap". Julie has the large bath towel to dry her doll because "my doll is the biggest". Julie holds the doll up high "to get all the water from inside her" and is fascinated to watch it stream out from a little hole in the doll's big toe. She dried her off well and said, "She can't have two washes".

4 The Family

Introduction

When a three- or four-year-old child first comes to school, his real concern could almost be said to be his own identity. He is busy learning about himself, and at the same time finding out something about the world beyond his home and family, about other children, other adults and other things.

In general young children need to feel important; they are proud of their own achievements and proud and possessive of their own property. The school provides freedom of choice and the encouragement to experiment in play. Children love to discover that they can "do" something new, and through the provision that is made and suggestions that are offered, each child is able to succeed at his own level. Most of the child's talk about himself, his toys, the things that he has seen or those he can do, arises spontaneously from his play. Talk and activity centred on the child himself are likely to encompass mathematical ideas naturally, and some of these are explored in the section "Myself", below.

The child's willingness to talk about his family and his home, however, will be much more likely to reflect his own individual circumstance. Some children have considerable difficulties at home. It is certainly not intended that intrusion of any kind should be encouraged into an area of the child's experience which must be sensitively respected, and this must be kept in mind when reading the section "My family".

In some communities the extended family is the child's experience, and although some examples involve primarily the "nuclear" family, these will extend to include cousins, uncles, grandparents as appropriate.

The section, "The family", is perhaps more likely to be explored in terms of an imaginary one—the family in a story or rhyme, or the family of dolls that lives in the doll's house. Here there are established relationships, sizes and perceptible properties which might be talked about, without offending any child.

In the next section some of the circumstances in which mathematical ideas have occurred, from talk and activity about families, are discussed. They are given as an indication of what can happen and a suggestion of some of the ways in which similar ideas might be explored by different children in different circumstances.

1 Myself: e.g. I'm growing; my birthday; look in the mirror; hands and feet; dressing up; it's mine; I can and I can't; making things to fit.
2 My family: e.g. who's tallest?; how many; our pets; it looks like; my house; things we use at home; comparisons; ordering; baking; creative work and painting.
3 The family: e.g. dolls; other toys; stories and rhymes; "happy families".

Possible developments

Myself

"I", "me" or "mine" are words that are frequently heard in the classroom, as a child proudly announces that he has "built a big tower" or "got one like that", or as he asserts himself by virtue of possession, "That's mine". Such remarks can be an invitation to the teacher to come and listen or look, and as she shares the children's enjoyment and pride or helps them to sort out their problems, there are times when this will involve ideas which are mathematical.

I'm growing

Example
This was a conversation overheard at the lunch table:

Roger (5.1):   I got more hair than you, Rodney.
Rodney (4.4):   That's 'cos my head is growing.
Roger: My *hair* grows.
Rodney: Everything grows.
Josephine (4.4): Houses don't grow.
Roger: Babies grow.
Stephen (4.0):   Simon and me were babies.
Josephine: Lizzie and I were too. Do you know why Lizzie is bigger than me? 'Cos she was born first.

It is difficult for children to understand the process of growing. The common confusion of age with height is just one example (see chapter 11 *The Passage of Time*). "When I'm big" is a favourite thought.

Example
Anna (4.3):   When I'm six I will be much bigger. I will be a lady—no, I will have to be bigger still more.
James (4.2):   When I'm grown up big I shall be like a giant, and I shall be up here and I shall look down at you and you will say, "What are you doing up there?"

With help, "big" is gradually replaced by "older" or "taller" as these different ideas acquire meaning.

Often there are two tiers of coat pegs for the children to use and many who "can't quite reach" when they first come to school, can use them easily two or three terms later.

Sometimes a teacher considers it suitable to help some of the children make marks on the wall to establish their present height, and these marks are then compared with others made later in the term (perhaps in a different colour) so that children can see how much they have grown. Lengths of wool or strips of paper are sometimes used to emphasise that the mark represents a height from the floor.

"I'm as tall as the tower."

Children for whom this activity may have little meaning can compare their own height with towers of blocks, tops of cupboards and so on. For them the comparison must be immediate.

Comparing the heights of two children in the group or ordering several can be a spontaneous and useful activity, again using ideas of taller and shorter, the tallest and the shortest. On the other hand, as a group activity it can be less than enjoyable for the shortest child in the group if he is continually identified as "the shortest", when he needs to believe that "he's a big boy, really".

Children often notice differences in size when they play, when, for instance, they fit themselves under a table or try to crawl through a hoop.

Of course a child's comments need not always be explored but are of themselves tremendously important in giving an indication of his stage of thinking.

Examples

Ann-Marie (3.6): I am bigger than her, she not smaller than me.

Ceri (4.2): My mum is buying me a new bathing suit. The one I had last year is too small—'cos I've grown bigger.

Vocabulary: older than – younger than – taller than – shorter than – oldest – youngest – tallest – shortest.

My birthday

The celebration of each child's birthday in school can involve other ideas than "how old am I?" which is explored in chapter 11 *The Passage of Time*. Each class will have its own birthday rituals which offer the children different experiences.

When children help to put out chairs for the group or distribute mugs of orange juice or bottles of milk, then they need to establish one-to-one correspondence. They may find that there are more children than chairs, for instance, and have to find how many more chairs are needed to provide one each.

It may be that the baking group will make "birthday biscuits" and the baking and distribution will involve mathematical ideas. Sometimes a cake may be sent to school for the children to share; sharing a cake for a large group of children would not be done by the children themselves, though it might turn into a spontaneous counting activity. "How many of us are there? Let's count. How many pieces will we need?" These will then be given out one to each child.

Sometimes the class has a permanent "birthday cake". The child can then put the same number of candles on it as his years, perhaps putting "how many for last year?", "four" and then one more for his "fifth" birthday. If the candles are to be blown out there may be talk about the number extinguished at one blow, for example, "Three have gone out – two more to go!"

If a child brings in his birthday cards, then the teacher might explore his interest by talking with him about the number of cards, the pictures (colours, sizes, what's happening, etc.), the shape and size of the cards, and the number symbol. Talk might identify similarities and differences and lead to simple comparisons or ordering. Through this personal talk, the teacher avoids any competitive feeling that might occur if this became a group activity.

Vocabulary: one each – more – fewer – older – younger – one – two – three – four – five – third – fourth – fifth.

Look in the mirror

The mirror, especially a full length one, can provide plenty of fun when children pull funny faces or make different shapes. Without inhibiting this enjoyment, there may be occasions when attention can focus on comparisons such as longer, wider, taller, as children experiment.

The mirror can be useful in checking whether one child is taller than another in such a way that both can clearly see the difference. Looking at his reflection a child sees that he has two eyes and one nose, that his mouth is lower than his nose, his ears are at each side of his head.

Angled mirrors can be fun ("Look where his arms come out now") and provide experience of symmetry.

A child can also see more easily the one-to-one correspondence of the buttons and button holes on his coat. If he is asked to count the buttons on his shirt or see how many colours are in the pattern of his sweater, then a look in the mirror might help with this too.

Vocabulary: taller than – shorter than – wider than – narrower than – curved – straight – next to – underneath – behind – above – looks like.

Hands and feet

Example
Fiona (4.7) said to Jason (4.10), "Your boots are on the wrong feet."
Teacher: How do you know?
Fiona: They are facing in the wrong direction.

Children are often asked to use their own bodies for counting and corresponding. How many eyes, hands, feet, legs, toes, fingers? How many shoes do we need for our feet or gloves for our hands? And, of course, they notice when shoes don't fit or there's one missing.

"I've lost my shoe."

Comparisons of the size of hands or feet often occur spontaneously, or are prompted by a visit to a shoe shop or making handprints in wet sand, wet footprints by the paddling pool and so on.

Prints may be made of hands spread or with fingers close together. Footprints might be made in different directions; "sideways", "forwards", "backwards". Comparison of size might be made more clearly between prints made by an adult and those made by the children.

Hands and feet are used to print with paint or into clay or damp sand. They might be printed in pairs or in patterns which repeat. When more than one child's prints are made, then the sizes may be compared or ordered. Sometimes children try to print with just one thumb or finger, or two fingers or three fingers.

Dressing up

The clothes that the children wear or dress up in often prompt comment. Children like to show off new clothes and new toys for that matter, and may enjoy the opportunity of talking with an adult about colour, patterns, when or where bought or made, and so on.

"The ladybird has spots – just like my dress! They're circles."

Some will enjoy looking round the class for things that are the same colour, or might like to try to copy the pattern of a simple fabric, if provided with similar shapes and colour paints to enable them to experiment. They might go on to sort similar materials from the scrap material box, perhaps sorting all the floral designs or all the striped pieces. The full length mirror can be a great help by enabling the child to look at things he is wearing which he may be trying to describe.

Children often claim similarity, and experience of comparison will enable them, like Tom, to explore whether things are exactly the same or not.

Example

Andrew (4.11) and Tom (4.6) were sitting drinking milk.

Andrew: Hey, we have both got the same socks. They are long ones.

Tom: Yes, they are the same but yours are a bit different. They are slightly darker grey and you've got a different pattern on yours.

Andrew: Yes, but they are the same.

Children are not always concerned with the size of clothes in which they dress up and the teacher would not intrude in any imaginative role play through an inappropriate concern for mathematics. Children do occasionally comment on the length of dresses though, and have to solve the problem of the dress that is too long for them to walk in, or the jacket which is too small.

It's mine

Example

Shafgar (4.1) was showing his paintings to the teacher. He said, "I done another one. Two paintings. I'll take these two paintings home.

It is sometimes difficult for children to remember which things are theirs or were made by them. Beginning to take responsibility for their own property, they may be proud to count how many paintings they have done or sort their work from the pile, to take home.

The use of personal symbols in many schools, provides each child with a sense of what is his. This is his peg and his coat must be put on it. This is his symbol to place on a bottle of milk to show that it is his. This idea establishes a one-to-one relationship of "belonging".

Young children may lay claim to possession just because they happen to be playing with, say, a car or doll. Sharing can cause problems, but in some cases the children can be encouraged to explore possible solutions for themselves. An example is given in Example 1 later. Their pride of possession can confuse ideas of size. Some children tend to insist that their models, cars, towers, etc. are the biggest, fastest or tallest and it is not always kind to suggest otherwise. Others are much happier to have their judgements explored and can check their claims.

I can and I can't
Experiment and activity enable children to find out about things that they can and cannot do. Often their comments or explanations involve mathematical ideas like height, weight, shape or space.

Example
Nigel (4.8):   (Balancing along a plank) "Look, I can balance all the way along here.
Teacher: Can you tell me what balance means?
Nigel: Mind you don't fall off.

Nigel had invited his teacher's attention and in turn she had offered him a chance to try to tell her what he meant by "balance".

Example
Donna (3.10):   (On the swing) I can't push myself.
Teacher: No, your feet don't touch the ground.
Donna: But the swings in the park are smaller. I can push myself on those.

It would be difficult to explore the idea of "smaller" as Donna has used it. They may be smaller; they may just be nearer the ground. At any rate she has noticed the difference and tried to describe it.

Making things to fit
Making things to fit the children themselves can be tricky, and children will probably need the help of a friend or an adult.

Example
The teacher joined a group of three who were spontaneously cutting and pasting paper crowns for themselves. Robert (4.1) made his and the teacher said, "It doesn't quite fit, does it?" Donna (5.0) interrupted saying "You should have done it bigger [for longer] like me. I'll do you one."

Experience will teach Robert that it is more efficient to make an estimate first—"This length fits round my head. I'll use this one."

My family

Each child's home circumstance is different, and not all children will want to talk about it in school. The child's willingness to share his news and to talk about his family should not be inhibited for the sake of any mathematical ideas that might be incidental to it. There are times when these ideas will occur naturally and when it will be appropriate, and this is for the child's teacher to decide.

Who is the tallest?
Children talk about size as "big" rather than using finer definitions like "tall" or "wide" or "long". It must be difficult for them to understand when the way that we use "big" is so confusing.

Example
Teacher: How big is your new baby?
Amy (4.11):   He isn't big, he's small.
Andrew (4.8): Mummy's biggest. I'm smallest, but I'm a big boy.

Very young children may find little meaning in the question of who is the tallest in your family.

Example
Ayeshea (3.6):   I'm biggest. Bigger than Lucy (elder); bigger than mummy and daddy.

Usually, we assume that dad will be the tallest, mum the next tallest and so on, but of course this may not be so and unless we know the family there may be little point in exploring the idea. Comparisons are best made at this early stage between things which the children can see.

When talking about brothers and sisters, children can often say who is the tallest or shortest, but find it difficult to distinguish between oldest and youngest. Again they prefer to say "I've got a big brother" or "a little sister". In some families there may be little distinction made between siblings and cousins, and these may be included in any discussion.

Ideas of height and age are best explored using things in the class or the children themselves. Then gradually their

experience will enable them to make sound judgements about their family.

Example
Emily (4.0):   Mummy is the oldest. Daddy is taller, but that doesn't mean he's older.

How many?
Sometimes children like to list the names of the members of their family and in this way we can help them to count how many there are, and help them to remember to include themselves in the count!

Our Pets
Family pets may be included in the child's idea of his family. Pets which are kept in school can reinforce this interest and there are many incidental mathematical experiences involved in their care—water containers may be filled and emptied, more water may be needed, or a certain number of leaves may be fed to the pet and so on.

Caring for the class pet might prompt the child to comment on his own pet. Talk might involve ideas of comparison of shape, size, colour or weight. Pictures might be found in books which "look like" the family pet, and these could be discussed.

It looks like
Children enjoy finding things in school which look like those at home. The interest which this kind of discovery sparks off can often lead to some finer comparison: "Is it exactly the same? How is it different?"

Examples
Andrew (4.4):   I want that box because it looks like my daddy's car.
Andrew has been prompted to make a model car like his dad's.

Lee (4.8) :   My daddy has two vans, a blue one and a yellow one. Daddy goes to work in them. One is a big one and one is a little one.

Lee's spontaneous remark could have been followed by a suggestion that he tried to sort the vans from the other vehicles in the garage, or he could have been encouraged to watch vans travelling outside the school. A natural follow-up would be for him to make a model van, perhaps like one of his dad's. Ideas of speed might be introduced; his dad's van goes faster than the toy van in the garage. Watch the traffic outside for things that move fast or more slowly; the cars might be counted and compared for size, shape or colour.

My house

Children might recognise similarities between the house or flat in which they live and one illustrated in a book or noticed on a visit. The discussion which follows may involve comparison and the use of various mathematical ideas. Models or paintings might be made and perhaps become a similar basis for talk. For obvious reasons it would be unwise to encourage children to make comparisons between their respective homes.

Things we use at home

Collections can be made of things that we use "in the garden" or "in the kitchen", for instance. They could include Home Corner equipment, pictures from magazines or objects from a furnished doll's house.

Reorganising the Home Corner can involve sorting of this kind, putting things for the kitchen in one area and things for the bedroom in another. Discussion might arise, for instance, about the saucepans in the Home Corner. Are the ones at home like that? How are they different? The children might have made a collection of shiny things or things made of metal, and be invited to think of things that they use at home which are shiny or made of metal.

Comparison

Children make use of family terms to make comparisons of size.

Example

David (3.7) was playing on the slide. He said, "It's just right for me, but mummies and daddies can't go on it, can they?"

The language of comparison (taller, shorter, longer, wider, higher, stronger . . .) acquires meaning through its use in many contexts. It may be that David's teacher would consider it appropriate to wonder why he thought mummies and daddies couldn't go on the slide. Is it "too narrow"? Would they be "too heavy"?

Ordering

Sometimes when children put more than two people or objects in order, they also make use of "family" terms, giving the teacher the chance to introduce correct vocabulary.

Example

Catherine (4.7) was playing with four balls of clay.

Catherine :   The biggest, the girlest, the boyest, the smallest. (She then changed to . . .) Daddy, could be mummy, then the boy and next the baby.

Again one might choose to introduce the mathematical terms—larger, smaller, look the same. It may be that Catherine is giving her clay balls identities rather than deliberately ordering them.

Baking

Example
Fiona (4.7) made four biscuits and took them home. The next day she said, "I couldn't give one to daddy because there weren't enough. I had one, Justin had one, Joanna had one and mummy had one, so I gave daddy a bit of mine."

Making biscuits in school to take home to her family had given Fiona an opportunity to share her biscuits, and a chance to share school and home experience. Informal fractions (see chapter 7 *Towards Number* often occur in conversations of this kind.

Vocabulary: one each – the same – more – fewer – smaller – half – quarter.

Creative work and painting
Children like to make models or collage pictures of their home, and the enjoyment of the activity should not be lost to our concern for form and detail. It is enough to know that the children are able to experiment freely with space and shape, and without necessarily feeling a need to talk about it. There is a lot to be learnt from standing back and observing the way a child plays with shape and form, but it may be that the child will want to talk about it afterwards, or ask for help to find particular shapes of materials as he works.

Children also like to paint their family or part of it, but they do not necessarily show the correct number in the family or reflect gradations in size. The boy who has no dad, for instance, may paint dads all over the place; the one with a new baby sister may leave her out altogether.

Sometimes children make things to take home for particular members of their family. This is a link between home and school and might stimulate talk about numbers, size and relationships.

Young children need to have freedom of expression in their art work and it should not be sacrificed for the sake of an exercise in counting or comparison.

The family

Dolls
Families of dolls or puppets provide children with the opportunity for much free imaginative play. The doll family can also be the basis for exploring ideas of relationships, comparison, ordering and number. Mr and Mrs X and their children live in the house in the corner by the books. Here they are:

Mr X   Mrs X   Girl   Boy   Baby

They are all different. When the children meet the family some of the differences might be pointed out; others the children may notice as they play.

Of those standing, Mr X is the tallest. Girl is the shortest. (Though baby is smaller still.)
Their clothes are of different textures and patterns.
Mr X has long trousers whilst Boy has shorter ones.
Which of the family are wearing something green?

The family may have a well-furnished house, with furniture of different sizes for each member, so the children may use each size appropriately.

Relationships in general are important in mathematics (see chapters 1 and 2 *Space and Shape* and *Comparisons*). Exploring relationships within the family is yet another opportunity for this experience—for example, Mr X is the father of Boy, Boy is the son of Mr X. The doll family can, of course, be extended to include "grandparents", "aunts" or "cousins", as thought suitable.

Perhaps some children would be able to make new "clothes" for the family; things that fit. (Clothes of different size and type can be sorted.) They might like to make a family of their own with fewer members, and a simple house in which they can live. This will include ideas of space and shape.

Vocabulary: taller than – shorter than – tallest – shortest – oldest – youngest – younger than – older than – looks like – longer – same as – straight lines – circles – all – some – fits – too long – too short – too small – wide – long – tall – across – above – next to – together.

Other toys
Of course the family need not be "human". One might improvise a family of fishes or cars or imaginary creatures. The imaginary ones might have a different number of legs or eyes, some with tails, others without. They will be different sizes (length, width, height) and may be of different colours or patterns. This will provide opportunity to notice similarities and differences. Again the family may be introduced through an improvised story, perhaps one which involves attention to comparison in some way. Homes of suitable shape and size might be made for each individual creature.

Stories and rhymes
Traditional stories are a great source of enjoyment, and those like "The Three Bears" include mathematical ideas which might be explored in talk and creative work. (See also chapter 12 *Rhymes and Stories*.) A small table might be set out for the three bears' breakfast with three sizes of chair, bowl and so on, together with three sizes of bear for the children to play with.

Although children become familiar with the terms used in the story and call out when they are listening to it, the ideas involved may not necessarily have been understood. Again it is important for children to experience these ideas practically in a variety of ways to enable them eventually to achieve full understanding.

The teacher's role

As always, it is the role of the teacher to be aware of the possibilities for helping children to explore mathematical ideas. "The Family" relies very heavily on the teacher's skill in realising the importance of listening to children talking and also knowing when simply to listen and when to listen and suggest or question.

The teacher does have a role in initiating interest and activity through the use of dolls, pictures, rhymes or stories, and in pursuing any teaching point when she feels it is right to do so. The teacher who finds, for instance, that a child has difficulty in including himself in a "family count up", may make sure that he has opportunity for counting the members of many different groups of which he is a part, on other occasions.

Here are some examples of ways in which individual teachers have explored particular comments or happenings.

In the first example given below the teacher is quick to follow Bruce's initiative, and to ask him to suggest a way of sharing. At no point does she tell Bruce that his idea was wrong. Instead, she guides him to check his suggestion and when he realises that he is not successful, she skilfully involves him in the final solution to the problem.

Example 1
This story involves Mona (3.3) and Kim (3.6), and also Bruce (5.1), who is visiting from another class. Bruce and Kim have large lumps of clay. Mona walks up and grabs Kim's lump.

Bruce: She's taken Kim's.
Kim: Gimme.
Mona: Mona's, Mona's. (She speaks little English.)
Teacher: Give it back to Mona and we'll find some for you.
Kim: Gimme.
Bruce: Let's share it.
Teacher: How shall we do that?
Bruce Mona can have half of mine and half Kim's. (He cuts approximately half from each and gives them to Mona.)
Kim: Her got lots.
Bruce: No, she's got half.
Teacher: Are you sure, Bruce? What did you give her?
Bruce: I gave her half of this and half of this.
Teacher: Put your bit beside hers.
Bruce: It's bigger. I know, we'll put it in one big lump and you can share it.
Teacher: How many people want a lump?
Bruce: One, two, three.
Teacher: So I'll cut it into thirds. You can have one third each, not one half, like this. Now, does that seem fair?
Bruce: Look, they are the same!

In the next example, does Nichola imply that she believes her feet to have stopped growing now? Her teacher would know whether the idea of "growing" is one that confuses Nichola, and would know whether or not to pursue the idea on another occasion. The teacher might, however, go on to invite comparison between, for instance, the new sandals and the old shoes, or the size of Nichola's feet and her own.

Example 2
Nichola (3.7):

Look at my new sandals, teacher—they're the next size up! My feet had grown and the man said my shoes were too small so now I'm going to wear my sandals *all* the time. I'm glad my feet grew!

"I'm glad my feet grew!"

In the following example the teacher has quite deliberately sought to initiate interest in the comparison of ages and heights, by arranging for older brothers and sisters to visit the group. Knowing her children, the teacher had decided that this activity was suitable for them. In each case the teacher tried to encourage the use also of "opposites"; Steven is *taller than* Linda—Linda is *shorter than* Steven.

Example 3
The children invited older brothers and sisters from another school to visit the group. They looked at each family separately.

These are some of the ideas which were mentioned on that occasion and which will be met in many other different contexts, leading towards a real understanding of them.

Steven is *taller than* Linda.
When Linda stands on a chair Linda is *higher than* Steven.
Steven is *older than* Linda.

Heather and Anita are the *same size* although Heather is *older than* Anita.

Bernie is a *little taller* than Elizabeth.

Adrian is *much taller* than Davie.

Sharon is *older than* Tracey. When Sharon stands on a chair, Tracey is *lower than* Sharon.

Karen is *taller than* Mark and Mark is *taller than* Martin.
Mark is *older than* Karen and Karen is *older than* Martin.
Karen is the tallest.
Martin is the shortest.
Mark is in the middle.

5 Water

Introduction

Water is fascinating and exciting to all children. For many of them, the classroom will be the first place where they are able to play with water and even spill it on the floor without incurring an adult's displeasure. Mops and cloths should be provided so that children can mop up their own spills, and so help to prevent accidents.

Running water from taps, plug holes and drains are all things to be explored, as are ditches, puddles, fish tanks and the pets' water containers.

"Where *does* that water go?"

It is not easy to follow a child's thoughts as he pours, fills and empties. He could be working something out, but he may just be enjoying emotional relaxation and a purely sensory level of play. The water trough can then be a peaceful place where children make social contact with other children and adults and talk of many things. At other times it is suddenly exciting, as a new discovery is made or a sensitive teacher initiates a new game just as the last activity begins to pall.

Given a free choice, children usually choose the apparatus they are ready for and although a three-year-old may imitate the feats of an older child with a funnel, tube and bottle, he may not gain the same satisfaction as he does from achieving something much more simple on his own.

The child who has been moving boats and other objects that float on the surface of the water, suddenly discovers that he can make them sink by holding them down or pouring water on top of them. Next he may discover that containers full of water will stand on the bottom of a trough of shallow water. He continues pouring from one container to another, and after lots of experience and conversation with the adults around him can begin to estimate how much he is going to need to fill the guinea pig's water bowl or top up the vase of flowers. Younger children often try to use a funnel as a scoop, but as they progress, it is used to fill bottles, control the flow of water through the water wheel and as part of a complex water system of pipes, jugs and bottles on different levels.

Children make progress at various speeds at different ages and by watching their activities and offering the next stage when they are ready for it teachers can give them the breadth of experience that will make the formal work of later years more meaningful. Valuable mathematical experiences need not be confined to the well-ordered water trough, and the sensitive adult can find many ways of introducing new vocabulary and mathematical ideas during the children's play.

Possible developments

Washing

a) There must be enough time and space for each child to wash properly. As there are often only half a dozen wash-basins, turns must be arranged and children soon realise that there are too many or not enough children for the basins available. Fitting in plugs and turning taps on and off may all be new experiences, as well as estimating how much water is needed. Will the water overflow if two hands are plunged into the bowl? What happens to the overflowing water and also to the waste water? If a mother can bring a baby to be bathed, there will be valuable conversation about temperature, displacement and the sequence of washing, rinsing, drying and dressing.

b) Tablecloths, mats, napkins, dolls' clothes, dressing up clothes, cot and pram covers all need to be washed at various intervals and provide experiences of sorting, displacement, comparison, absorption and evaporation.

Young children can be helped to plunge, rub and squeeze, and if a wringer or spin dryer is used (by an adult, of course), the children will be amazed to see how much more water can be extracted than by just squeezing.

c) The cups, saucers, pots and pans in the Home Corner all need washing at intervals. In fact, if there is an un-carpeted area, real water can be used in the play sink or a bowl, and "meals" can be followed by real washing up, sorting and restacking in cupboards or on shelves.

d) Regular washing of plastic bricks and toys helps to

"Shall we try to push them all under the water?"

preserve their freshness and while standard Lego pieces can be soaked in a small bowl, larger bricks will need a larger container. The bricks and other plastic toys then need to be sorted and fitted back into their appropriate containers. Dolls can be bathed and the correct sequence (as for the real baby) encouraged.

e) Pastry boards, rollers, cutters and cooking tins all need washing. Offer the children different materials for drying up. The children can sort which absorb most water.

Vocabulary: too many – not enough – how much? – inside – outside – underneath – on top of – sort – under – over.

Indoor and outdoor gardens

a) Probably one of the easiest ways to show that water is necessary, is to germinate cress seeds on wet blotting paper, cotton wool, flannel, etc. Children can watch them absorb the water, grow fatter and begin to shoot. Daily additions of water will maintain the growth. Peas and beans can be grown in jars, supported by damp paper; carrot and parsnip tops grow in saucers of water; onions, potatoes and hyacinths resting on the top of jars of water will send roots down and make top growth; cuttings such as Busy Lizzie and Tradescantia will produce roots when standing in water. Controls can be set up for most of these experiments, e.g. plant cress seed on *dry* botting paper as well as wet, so that children begin to realise that it really is the water that is responsible for the change.

b) There is a need for daily or weekly watering of pot plants and the effect of too much or too little water is soon evident. As bulbs grow in pots, the amount of water needed varies according to the growth of the flowers. Flowers and vegetables grown outdoors need regular watering in hot weather. Routine and quantity can be established.

c) Cut flowers in vases need the water changed or topped up. Size and quantity of flowers for vases can be estimated and experimented with.

Vocabulary: up – down – through – under – over – too much – too little – weekly – daily.

Cooking

a) Where a refrigerator is available (or in freezing conditions outside), flavoured ice cubes or lollies can be made. Discuss the shape of containers and whether they should be full or nearly full. Melting, and the size of container needed to hold the liquid afterwards, can also be explored.

b) Use water to mix real pastry, icing sugar or play dough.

c) Cold drinks can be made by diluting concentrated squash or mixing water with powder. Share the mixture between cups. Estimate how many cups can be filled or try to pour equal quantities into a given number of cups.

d) Feel the different textures of sugar, salt, flour, etc. Try mixing each with a little water. Which dissolve? Which form a paste? Which are unaffected?

e) Soak dried fruit, peas, beans, etc. before cooking them. Discuss how much water is necessary—too much or too little. Leave an equal amount of fruit unsoaked, so that children can compare the difference in size and weight.

Vocabulary: full – empty – half full – add – mix – share – how much? – too much – little – enough.

Pets

Children can often help to refill drinking containers for their pets, and bird baths. Further uses of water in the care of pets can be found in *Small Mammals* (Wray, J. D. *Small Mammals*, Schools Council Project Educational Use of Small Animals, English Universities Press Ltd., 1974).

Vocabulary: deep – shallow – round – flat – inside – outside – full – empty – too much – enough.

Rainy days

a) Watch the raindrops on the windows. Do they run down, joining together or are the blobs separate? Paint a blob-and-trickle picture using watery paint on smooth or textured paper on an easel.

b) Watch raindrops falling into puddles and look for circles of various sizes. Raindrops feel and look heavy when they hit us or the ground. Where have they come from? Listen to the rain. Compare slow dripping, fast gushing, trickling, etc.

c) Look for drips from gutterings or a leaky roof. Catch them in a bucket. How soon will it be full or too heavy to carry?

d) Set up a simple "weather station" by collecting rain in a container. Is there more today than yesterday?

e) After it has been raining, go out in rubber boots to look for puddles, and walk through them. Notice how the footprints fall, their pattern, size, etc.

f) Ride through puddles on bicycles, tricycles, trucks, etc. Notice different tyre marks and number of tracks. Find out how to make straight or curved tracks.

g) Look at the size of the puddles, chalk round them, cut string to stretch round them or use small bricks to surround them. Look again later—has evaporation made them smaller or has more rain made them bigger? Jump or step over puddles, estimating size.

Paddling pools

a) Boats of varying sizes and weights can be floated in a pool while children paddle, but some objects will sink. Does the depth of water affect this?

b) In a swimming pool, rubber rings, balloons, etc. float. How can you tell if the water is deep? In which part can a child/adult stand on the bottom?

c) A sprinkler or hose will show fragmentation and many colours in the sun.

d) If buckets are used to fill the pool, they can be counted and discussions about empty and full will develop as water is transferred from one to the other.

Vocabulary: float – sink – empty – full – in – out – under – on top of – deep – shallow.

Rivers, streams, ponds and seashore

These are all potentially dangerous areas, and although many interesting discoveries can be made, children must be carefully supervised and not allowed to explore alone.

a) Ways of crossing rivers and streams can be discussed; bridges, stepping stones, rafts and boats. But this is only practical if expeditions with teachers and parents can be planned to give children first-hand experience. What can be found in the stream? Notice the different speeds of movement of snails, fish, tadpoles, etc. Why do our paper boats always float that way? Is the water flowing up-hill or down-hill? Do leaves, twigs or stones float? What happens when the water freezes?

b) On the seashore, gullies can be dug for the incoming tide to fill. Water can be seen to seep away from holes or fill up holes as it finds it own level.

c) Ponds can be watched for reflections on still water, sunlight sparkling and ripples caused by the wind. A straight stick held in the water will appear to bend, showing refraction.

d) Discuss the open sea, fast flowing water in waterfalls, mountain streams and potholes, water in reservoirs behind a dam and the fresh water in our taps. These topics may all be within some children's experience.

Vocabulary: over – through – under – behind – up – down – fast – slow – full – empty.

Water troughs, trays and bowls

Although children will already have had everyday experiences with water this may be the first time that water has been offered to them as a material to play and experiment with. The tray should be in a part of the room that can be mopped up easily, but not isolated from the rest of the children and adults in the group.

The equipment, which should be stored nearby, can be sorted on to shelves or into bins and buckets. These could be labelled with pictures as well as words so that some children can match and sort for themselves. Different selections of equipment will encourage children to experiment in different ways, and a plank resting over the tray will make a level surface on which to stand containers to be filled. The selection can be varied with some of the following activities in mind.

a) Drop corks, stones, shells, pieces of coal, wood and sponge into various depths of water. Play with hollow boats, solid and hollow figures, balls and containers that will float when empty but sink when full. Sort out objects according to whether they float or sink. Do all small objects float and large ones sink?

b) Use pipes, bottles, buckets and the water-wheel to find out about the force of water and the direction of flow. Fill and squeeze plastic bottles to show propulsion.

c) Pour water into and through sieves, colanders and yoghurt pots with holes pierced in the sides or bottoms. Try to fill paper, cloth bags or cardboard boxes. How are they different from plastic pots?

d) Provide varying sizes of jugs, buckets and bottles. Many children feel the need to pour from one container to another continuously as they slowly acquire manual skill.

e) Provide containers of various shapes which hold approximately the same amount. Assorted plastic bottles can be cut to the appropriate size. Children will begin to see that the same amount of water will fill containers that appear to be of different capacity. The original amount (with care!) remains constant.

f) Provide a set of cups or beakers of similar size and shape to give experience of sharing, estimating and matching.

g) Provide pots that can be half-filled with water and then have stones dropped into them so that children can see the water level rising and find out about displacement.

h) Use scraps of soap, liquid soap or soap flakes shaken up in the water to make bubbles. Provide a separate bowl of diluted steriliser in which to rinse pipes and tubes. Use tubes of varying diameters and lengths, and special bubble pipes. Drinking straws are best avoided, as children are more used to sucking than blowing through them.

i) Provide translucent pots with lids, that can be half-filled with coloured water, to find out about the movement of water and its level, despite the tilting of the pot.

Vocabulary: full – empty – share – solid – hollow – sink – float – flow – through – up – down – over – under – fill – level.

The teacher's role

It is not enough just to provide the equipment and the opportunities; the relaxed and warm feeling must be created between adult and child that will help them both to enjoy making discoveries together. Many words which express mathematical ideas are used over and over again and it is important that they are used correctly, especially comparatives such as wider, longer, deeper, heavier, lighter, thicker and thinner.

Young children imitate and "play" the activities that they see adults enjoying. For example, a teacher who says that she thinks some of the dolls need bathing will soon have some willing helpers. Some of the following sentences are bound to occur during the doll-washing activity:

> Who will find the bowl for the water?
> Do you think that one is the right size?
> Let's see if the doll can sit in it.
> Do her legs bend, like ours?
> Will you get a jug and put some water in it?
> It's not too heavy for you to carry, is it? Perhaps a
>   smaller jug would be lighter to carry?
> What happens to the water when we put the doll into
>   the bowl?
> Was the bowl too full?

It is not suggested that the teacher should keep up a non-stop commentary or continually repeat the children's answers and comments for the benefit of the rest of the group. If children can be drawn into normal conversation with adults as they work together, the ideas and experience

"Is that enough water?"

which they assimilate will begin to have more meaning for them.

Pot plants and flowers that need regular watering will be watched carefully by the children if they are helped to do the watering, and they will be quick to tell us that the guinea pig's water pot is empty if they can refill it themselves. Again, it is almost second nature to use such expressions as "Don't give them too much". What does "too much" mean? Perhaps a certain amount for each plant could be decided upon and gradually the amount needed can be estimated by the children.

When cooking with the children we want to finish with something eatable, so we are likely to add the liquid carefully ourselves, but we could let children experiment with the play-dough and if they make the first lot too soggy, more flour and salt can be added without much trouble until they make a "workable" dough, and there can be plenty of conversation about too much, too little, a little more, a lot more and enough.

Situations which involve deeper water out of doors need very careful supervision, but a small group of children with an adult could visit a bridge to watch boats move underneath as cars and buses go over the top. They might make their own bridge over a very small stream or ditch and find out what will float underneath.

Children are sometimes asked to experiment with a collection of items made of various materials by placing them in water. They are then encouraged to notice and talk about what happens, e.g. a plastic boat floats, but if filled with water, it sinks; or paper is lighter than a stone, but when it is wet through, it sinks.

Playing with the classroom water trough, some children feel the need to fill, pour and empty continuously. If simple containers are put away to introduce sieves, for example, the children who have previously enjoyed filling and emptying will drift away. It would seem better to add one or two different pieces of apparatus and an extra trough so that new pieces can be explored in the company of old favourites. Then, by watching and joining in with the children's play, the balance of new and old can be altered as their interests change, without having everything in the water at once. This sort of awareness of the children's requirements is a key role for the teacher in most activities as she tries to anticipate and provide for the next stage in each child's development.

In the following example the teacher is drawing Raymond into an activity, in the hope that it will lead to further thought.

Example 1
Teacher asked Raymond (4.5) if he would like to help her water the plants.

Raymond: Why?
Teacher: Why would you think so?
Raymond: Because they would die if they didn't have water. I would die if I didn't have water. This one [plant] is very dry.
Teacher: How much will this little plant need?
Raymond: Just a little water because it is a small plant.

In the next example, the teacher could have developed this child's thinking by suggesting that they should find out if the boat would still float when carrying a smaller stone or if a larger boat could carry the stone they had.

Example 2
Gary (4.3): The boat floats, but it won't if the stone's in it.
Teacher: Why will it not float if the stone is in, Gary?
Gary: Because the stone is hard.
Teacher: What does the hard stone do to the boat?
Gary: It makes it heavy, and it sinks.

The next example shows that Aabida needs a great deal more experience before she will understand how liquids behave in various shaped containers. Piaget (Piaget, Jean, *The Child's Conception of Number*, Chapter I, Routledge & Kegan Paul, 1952) has described many experiments of this type with children of four years upwards and concluded that it was not until about the age of seven that children were able to see that a quantity of liquid remains constant although it appears to change when poured into different shaped containers.

Example 3

Aabida (4.5), playing with water, carefully filled a tall transparent plastic bottle.

Teacher: Can you pour all the water in your bottle into this jug?

Aabida: (Looking at the jug, then back at the bottle.) Yes.

She lifted the bottle shakily and with care poured the water into the jug. It began to flow over the top. She carried on pouring. She then stopped pouring, but made no comment.

Teacher: Have you any water left in your bottle?

Aabida: Yes.

Teacher: Is the jug full?

Aabida: Yes.

Teacher: Can you fit any more water into the jug?

Aabida: No.

Aabida continued pouring water into various containers at teacher's suggestion, but remained convinced that a taller container held more water than a shorter, fatter one.

Although there is no adult conversation in the next example, it is obvious that Jill was a sympathetic listener, letting Dean enjoy his experiences and learn from them.

Example 4

Dean (4.6) was talking to a student in the washroom.

Dean: Can I help wash the tablecloths? (Returning from playroom with five in his arms.) I've got them. (Puts them in sink and runs water. Pulls up chair to sit by low sink and turns up sleeves.) Watch this, Jill. When I go down on the tablecloths, the water runs over my hand. (After moving to laundry room and using spin dryer.) They have dried good, haven't they, Jill? (Picks up bowl containing tablecloths to carry them back.) It's not so heavy when they have dried.

In the following example, Siobham is gaining valuable experience in pouring and estimating under the teacher's guidance, in a practical situation.

Example 5

Siobham (4.6), during lunch, asked the teacher, "Can I pour the water, please?"

Teacher: Yes, Siobham.

Siobham half fills each glass in turn except one which she fills to the brim.

Teacher: Siobham, I think that glass has too much water in it. Pour some back into the jug.

This she did, gauging how much was left in the glass by the amount in the other glasses.

The teacher in the next example has supplied just enough information to start Jonathon on the road to discovery.

Example 6

Jonathon (4.7):   What is that, teacher?

Teacher: It's a water wheel. See what happens when you pour water on the top.

Jonathon: It goes round. (pointing to the wheel.)

Teacher: What happens when you pour the water slowly?

Jonathon: It goes slow.

The final story began when Jane painted a picture. Had she seen a plastic brick floating, or did she have to think of a name for her wavy line and enclosed shape?

Example 7

"It's a brick floating on the water."

Teacher: Tell me about your painting, Jane.
Jane (4.5):   It's a brick floating on the water.
Teacher: Oh! Do you think a brick would float on water?
Jane: Yes.

At this point, Mark (4.8), who was making a clay elephant nearby and had overheard this conversation, interrupted with a very disdainful, "No! Bricks don't float on water

Jane: They do.
Teacher: Shall we try and find a brick to see if it will float?

After a short search they found a half brick made of concrete and went over to the water through.

Teacher: Jane, would you like to put it in the water to see if it will float?

Jane put it in and of course it sank. She was disappointed but Mark triumphantly said, "I told you so!"

Teacher: · All right, Mark, would you like to try this brick and see if this sinks? (handing him a large, hollow wooden brick.)
Mark: It's floating. That's 'cause it's only light!
Teacher: Mark, go and get the heaviest wooden block that you can find.

When Mark returned with a large wooden block and discovered that it floated, he looked up and a slow smile crept over his face as he said, "It's a trick!"

Teacher: No it isn't, Mark, really. All wooden things float. Let's look in this bucket and see which of these things will float and which of them will sink.

They took down the bucket labelled "Buoyancy" and experimented with stones, shells, pieces of wood, metal bottle tops, forks, sponges, plastic boats and animals, plastic bobbins and two plastic cups, one of which sinks when filled with water and the other which floats just under the surface. When all these objects had been tested and discussed, they took them out and put them on the shelf in two groups: those that floated, and those that sank.

Teacher: I wonder why some things float and others sink?
Mark: I know why. It's 'cause they're stronger.
Teacher: What do you mean, Mark?
Mark: Well, bricks are stronger—like that big heavy stone. (pointing to one of the stones that we had tested.)

At this point, he started to take off his plastic apron, indicating that he had finished with water for the day, leaving a bemused teacher reflecting on the relationship of density to "strength".

6 Raw Materials

Introduction

In the classroom, very young children are encouraged to explore and become familiar with the variety of objects and materials which are provided. Most classrooms have a wealth of materials such as sand, clay and wood, and make collections of natural things like shells, leaves and pebbles, all of which can form the basis of much free play and experiment. Other materials, like paint, dough, paper of all sorts, cardboard, waste cartons, cloth of various textures, tin foil and plastic cannot be called "raw", but are basic materials which have been brought within the scope of this booklet.

The provision of a range of materials and the opportunity to handle them freely, enables a child to become familiar with their various properties. The perceptive adult can help him to identify some of these properties and introduce the appropriate mathematical vocabulary. However, it is necessary to emphasise that exploration of materials such as sand, clay, soil and wood for sheer delight, without the intervention of an adult, is extremely important and for some children lasts a long time.

Mathematics is the study of relationships, and as children explore, they begin to appreciate the relationship between one surface and another, one colour and another and between various tools and surfaces.

The introduction of new materials, or the suggestion of new ways to use familiar ones stimulates interest and prompts comparison and experiment. The choice and preparation of materials gives a teacher the opportunity to lead children towards certain experiences. She can also make sure that the more mature children have access to special tools and materials so that their creativity may progress. For example, whilst a younger child will stick paper, cloth, seeds and leaves apparently haphazardly onto a piece of paper, the more mature child may divide his paper by folding or making crayon lines and use scissors to cut materials to the size and shape he wants.

Sorting

When a child looks for a particular size box or a piece of material of a certain colour or texture, he is taking early steps towards sorting. The number of choices, say in box sizes or colours of material, can sometimes be limited by the teacher so that the youngest children are not discouraged from their natural urge to sort.

Possible developments

Sand

Ideally, children should be offered regular experience of both wet and dry, coarse and silver sand. Many schools are fortunate to have an outside sand pit as well.

Dry and wet sand
Without equipment the children are able to enjoy the sensation of handling the sand, whether wet or dry. They can hold, pour or push it about. Wet sand can be moulded, whilst dry sand is much more elusive. They may watch the sand shifting as they tunnel their hands into it. Children may discover that the covering of sand in the tray can be pushed to one side into a mound, yet will still push back to cover the tray. This is leading towards the idea of "invariance of mass"—there is still the same amount even though it has changed form.

Water can be added to the dry sand, so that children can experiment with "rivers", "moats" or "seas". They may mix the water in to use the sand wet. The presence of both wet and dry sand in the same tray might prompt comparison of what each type feels like or the way each behaves.

Wet sand can be moulded, either by hand or using buckets, spades or moulds. Comparisons of space, shape or size may be made as well as weight and number.

Impressions and patterns may be made in the wet sand, either by hand or with the tools available. The activities may be spontaneous or at the suggestion of the teacher.

Let's make another line that's straight like that one. Let's make a pattern with the things that make triangles.

Sand equipment
Sand equipment can be varied in much the same way as the teacher would vary the equipment at the water tray. Some equipment will be more suited to dry or wet sand, though it is sometimes interesting for the children to try using the funnel, for instance, with the wet sand, and comparison can be made of the way the different types of sand feel and behave.

Example
Maxine (4.10): Wet sand won't go through the funnel because it soaks up the water and sticks together.

Below are summarised some of the opportunities for mathematical experience which arise through the use of various equipment with dry and wet sand:

Dry sand
Spades, scoops and spoons of different size, shape or colour give opportunities for comparisons.

Buckets and other containers can lead to comparisons of size, shape, capacity and full/empty.

Funnels, sieves, colanders, salt and pepper shakers can be used to compare the way sand behaves when wet and dry.

Sand combs lead to experiences of space and shape.

Plastic tubing of different sizes provide opportunities for comparisons. Transparent containers show level.

The sand wheel can be used with wet or dry sand. It will spin at different speeds with *less* or *more* sand.

Simple scales give experience of balance, mass and comparison. They can be used with wet or dry sand.

Wet sand
Spades, scoops, spoons of different size, shape or colour give opportunities for comparisons.

Buckets and other containers lead to comparisons of size, shape, colour and capacity.

Moulds give experience of filling space, and also of shape and size.

Sand combs and pattern makers (e.g. potato masher, rolling pin, rake) lead to experiments with space and shape, and can be used for describing patterns and lines.

The sand table

Outdoor sand pit
The outdoor sand pit may include many of the activities already described and is dealt with more fully in chapter 9 *Outdoor Activities*.

Vocabulary: full – part full – empty – inside – outside – holds more than/less than – through – up – down – curved – straight – round – faster/slower than – more – less – looks like/different – around – under – on top of – behind – higher than – further than.

Collections

Collections of raw materials of all kinds can be the source of much interest and talk. Comparisons may be made of many different properties; shape, size, colour, texture, where the things were found, their use, scent, etc. Each collection will offer different properties and in any sorting activity the criteria chosen will mainly depend on the children themselves, though other qualities might be mentioned by their teacher.

Collections may be made quite spontaneously; a sudden gust of wind might produce an assortment of fallen leaves or petals to be gathered, as this teacher found:

Example
After our half term holiday most of the leaves had fallen from the trees here and in the park. There was much conversation about the leaves. We watched the gardeners sweeping them into piles and the children swept up the leaves too. We compared the sizes of the gardeners' brooms with our own. We counted the piles of leaves. We talked about the sizes and shapes of the leaves. Some children made leaf prints—sizes and shapes were discussed.

Collections may be made following a child's interest in say "shiny" things or from the teacher's suggestion, "Let's collect things that are made of wood" or "things with lines on". A table or display space set aside may encourage the children to sort out their collection.

Children often bring a new toy or special gift they have received to show their teacher and friends, and this may become the basis for a collection, as may something as simple as a pretty sweet wrapper or even an old shoe.

Sometimes collections are made by the teacher herself to introduce new and possibly unfamiliar things for the children to explore. Such an "investigation" table might include a selection from cogs, clocks, a plug, a kaleidoscope, spoons, magnets, a glass stopper, an old radio and weights.

The "button box" is, of course, an old favourite and one which retains its fascination and offers endless possibilities for sorting. The children in the following example were using a collection of beads, and their teacher decided to initiate an activity.

Example
Teacher: Can you make a necklace the same as mine?
(3 red, 3 green, 3 yellow, 3 blue)

Kelly (4.4) looked at it and silently counted the three red beads, took three out of the box and threaded them; the same with the green beads. When she came to the yellow and blue ones, she did not need to count the beads on the teacher's necklace, but simply picked up three together with one hand and threaded them. The finished necklace looked the same as the teacher's in spite of constant interruptions and distractions.

Vocabulary: looks the same/different – more – fewer – straight – curved – round – heavier/lighter than – together – inside – outside – larger than – longer than – wider than – narrower than – smaller than – under – on top of – next to.

Junk materials

Sorting
Many schools store their junk materials in such a way that children can sort the materials for themselves. The sophistication of the system varies according to the amount of space available. It might be as simple as two picture-labelled boxes, one for cuboids, the other cylinders. Some schools have a wealth of scraps stored in drawers labelled with examples of the material contained; silver foil on the "shiny things" drawer, sticky paper for the paper scraps. Children may sort with or without adult help when they bring things or when they pack them away.

Old sweet jars make good containers for material scraps. Different colours, perhaps already cut into small pieces by an adult, can be sorted by teachers and children ready for collage work.

Children may enjoy spreading out a large selection of junk materials on the floor, and exploring and experimenting with them with the teacher's active participation and help. This might turn into a game. "Let's find things that are longer than this" or "Let's find things that will roll". Sorting and tidying up is, of course, a valuable mathematical experience as well as a very necessary part of the activity.

Model making
When children are actually involved in making things they often do not need an adult, unless they encounter a real difficulty and need help to cut or find a particular shape or material not already available. Nevertheless, without interfering, an adult who is obviously interested in what they are doing can encourage them to talk about the choices they are making regarding size, shape and texture. It may be that they will enjoy an opportunity to talk about their models afterwards, perhaps how they were made, or comparisons of materials used, but this will

obviously depend upon the child. Mathematical ideas of space and shape and comparisons will have been involved in the making and the teacher may learn much from observation.

Example
Mark (4.5) had a tall thin box stuck to a cheese carton. He tried to balance it with the thin box as the base. This was not very steady and the model fell over.
Mark: I'll turn it over and see if it works.
It then stood easily and he chose a larger box and stuck his model on the top. Again he tried to make it stand with the thin box as the base and once again it fell over. This time he simply said "It doesn't work" and walked off to another activity.

Knowing the child, the teacher would decide whether or not to pursue the teaching point and encourage Mark to try again. There does seem to be a development from apparently aimless handling towards quite deliberate modelling, and the teacher will observe this in the development of the children's free play.

Children should be able to use junk materials freely. The kind of things that they make may reflect ideas that they encounter in stories, rhymes or visits. In this way the teacher stimulates experiment without directing it. By ensuring that a good variety of the right kind of materials are available, such as cotton reels or cheese boxes for wheels, she can enable any child to pursue a particular interest. Older children may be much more ready to improvise for themselves. The mathematical experiences involved may be explored in talk with the teacher afterwards.

Junk materials are sometimes used to make puppets. Some puppets are simple enough for the children to improvise for themselves once the teacher has introduced the idea. Often a group of children will work alongside their teacher and may produce similar puppets, but at another time they may use the technique more creatively. Ideas of space and shape, as children fit or match or choose shapes and so on, will be involved. Some classes have even pursued the interest and made instant "puppet theatres" using large junk boxes and other scraps for decor.

Collage
Collage work with paper shapes can involve ordering and sorting, especially if different textures, colours or sizes are provided. Squares, circles, triangles and rectangles soon become familiar terms when shapes are regularly used and talked about. Imitative collage, perhaps following a story like "The Three Billy Goats Gruff", might use simple gradation of size.

Scrap materials can be used for three-dimensional collage as well as model making. Polyfilla, alabastine or plasticine spread onto cardboard or wood provides a base for buttons, buckles, conkers, etc. to be pressed in. Sticks or twigs can be used for poles, and "chains" or necklaces suspended from "pole" to "pole". This may be a group effort in which children are able to join as they wish and do as much or as little as they choose.

"... and I made his toe."

Often a theme arises from a story or rhyme or following an outing to a farm or zoo. There will be considerable opportunity in this kind of shared activity to talk with the children as they play and for the teacher to discuss the mathematical ideas involved.

Texture and shape
For young children the most exciting part of the play with junk is probably feeling and choosing. Encouraged by the teacher's interest, they may notice differences in shape, texture and other properties, and will discover that "rounded things" roll and so on. Children like to handle scraps of material of different texture and thickness. Pieces of lace or net, for instance, are fascinating materials to handle and look through. They might even be stiffened with starch and painted over to leave a pattern.

Other opportunities
Further practical experiences with space and shape may be gained through play with junk boxes and other materials large enough for the children to sit in and use in imaginative play as trains or cars.

Some packaging cartons can be stored flat, then opened up to produce large three-dimensional shapes. Sides can be painted in different colours and lead to conversations about "inside", "outside", "underneath", "on top of".

There are, of course, many other ways of using junk materials which may involve ideas of number, shape or comparisons. One group spent a long time comparing the different notes or tones produced when tubes of different width and length were blown or spoken down.

Vocabulary: round – straight – curved – flat – looks like/ different – together – all – longer/shorter than – wider/ narrower than – lighter/heavier than – next to – on top of – under – higher/lower than – taller/shorter than – at the top/bottom – other way round.

Painting and printing

Painting
Paint is another material which children need to use freely and creatively. They enjoy painting for its own sake, and although adult interest provides encouragement, it is essentially a private activity.

Much incidental mathematical experience may be involved in the organisation and preparation, as well as the clearing away.

Example
Simon (4.2) was bringing a bucket of water to wash down the paint easels. He said, "Look, Sara, this isn't too heavy for me to carry now."

Teacher: Why isn't it too heavy, Simon? (When last seen he was struggling.)
Simon: Because me and Sara (3.11) took some water out."

The provision of a variety of tools, paints or papers is one way in which teachers introduce the possibility of change and experiment while still leaving the children free to choose. Many schools, for instance, offer paper ready cut into a number of different shapes, and the children use whichever they want or need. Similarly, the colour of the paper provided may be varied and include dark colours as well as light ones. Paper of different texture or thickness may be used. The brushes, too, may be of different thicknesses or lengths.

The teacher is able to vary the ways in which the children make use of paint. Each variation can create opportunity for comparison to be made. The use of different implements, or the provision of different surfaces on which the paint is applied can lead to comparison of shape, size, texture, colour etc. The use of paint thickeners of various kinds (see page 94 Appendix A) and the mixing of the paint itself can involve comparison of colour and thickness as well as the idea of the time taken.

Of course these ideas will not be explored on each occasion and it is for the teacher to decide when it is right to pursue the child's interest.

Printing
Printing is another activity in which the teacher can create opportunity for attention to particular ideas. She might, for instance, put out a selection of objects for the children to print with, which will produce only different sized circles. As well as printing circles, the children might discover that it is possible to print a pattern of concentric circles, or print in sets of each size, or even make ordered sequences.

The use of three-dimensional shapes for printing gives opportunity for the shapes themselves to be compared and discussed.

 This brick, for example, can give a variety of prints, according to which surface is used.

e.g.

and a cheese box lid can produce

Example
Shelly (3.6): I'm going to use the bridge-shaped block. (Puts paint on the two square base areas.) Look, it doesn't look like a bridge any more. It looks like two squares.

Some children might be asked to predict the two-dimensional shape that will be produced from the three-dimensional shape.

Vegetables and fruits are often cut and used for printing. Potatoes, carrots and onions can be used, and other vegetables like cabbages and brussel sprouts also produce interesting sections and prints.

Hand and foot prints can be made and sizes compared.

Vocabulary: thicker/thinner than – looks or feels the same/different – longer/shorter than – wider/narrower than – heavier/lighter than – square – rectangle – triangle – circle – round – straight – curved – larger/smaller than – more/less than – more/fewer than – inside – outside – next to – under – above – all – some.

Modelling materials

Although materials like clay, dough, aloplast and plasticine have quite different qualities, they do all provide opportunity for mathematical experiences such as moulding the same amount into many different forms, sharing, or comparing size, shape, pattern and texture.

Once again it must be emphasised that creative play with these materials is tremendously important, and though mathematical experience may be an integral part of that activity, *the child's creative urge should never be sacrificed.*

Clay
Children will probably discover that patterns can be imprinted in the clay even without the provision of pattern-making tools. Their fingers will make an impression—as will the sleeve of their sweater!

Children need plenty of time to manipulate and mould with their hands before tools are introduced. Sometimes they can be given a lump of clay that is too heavy for them to lift and they will gain new experiences as they try to mould or divide it into pieces of a manageable size.

When rollers are set out, children may flatten the clay and use whichever shapes are provided, to press into the clay. This more deliberate pattern-making may be in imitation of the teacher's attempt or even at her suggestion.

"Pattern-makers", like potato mashers or meat hammers, may be provided for the children to use with the clay to produce different effects.

A loose consistency of clay can be used in an old forcing bag to pipe out lines and patterns. Lines may be curved, zig-zag or straight, for example, and blobs may be of different sizes.

Dough

Dough is a much used material in the nursery. Two simple recipes are included for the teacher in Appendix B on page 94. Teachers often invite the children to help with making the dough. The colour may be varied perhaps according to the type of tools put out with it; "natural" for pastry cutters and patty tins, for instance. Experience of different amounts, sharing and mixing will be enjoyed when children are able to share in the preparation.

Example

Several children were playing with the pastry and another child wanted to join in too.

Teacher: I wonder if Tracy could come and play, too. There doesn't seem to be any pastry left for her though; what do you think we could do?

May (4.0): Nothing. She'll have to wait until some-one's finished.

Carrie (4.5): No she won't. If we all give her a little of our pastry, she'll get a lot, and we'll have some left as well.

Children often use dough in imitation of pastry; rolling,

cutting and making cakes, pies or pasties. For this purpose, rolling pins, cutters of different shapes and sizes, and cake tins should be available. This play sometimes takes place in the Home Corner or café area and can provide experience of space and shape, comparisons and one-to-one correspondence.

Example

The teacher was sitting at the pastry table with several children. She rolled out the pastry and, using a small cutter, cut out seven small tarts and started to place them in a six-sectioned tart tin.

Geoffrey (4.9): You've made too many, teacher.

Teacher: How do you know that, Geoffrey?

Without saying a word, Geoffrey proceeded to place a tart in every section of the tart tin and then said, "See, there's one left."

The use of the material with no tools available is as important as ever; the dough can be stretched, broken and moulded into different shapes by hand. Once again, this gives experience of moulding the same amount into different forms.

Yoghurt cartons or cheese boxes may be put out as bases for the dough to be moulded onto as arms, legs, etc. Talk afterwards might explore similarity and difference and simple counting.

Smaller objects such as shells, buttons or bobbins may be provided to be used on any models produced, or as "print" makers to make impressions in the dough, providing experience of space and shape.

Plasticine

Plasticine is an old favourite and together with dough provides a useful alternative to clay.

Vocabulary: wider/narrower than – longer/shorter than – larger/smaller than – looks same/different – more/less than – more/fewer than – found – straight – curved – on top of – next to – underneath.

Wood

Although wood is not easy to obtain and certainly not cheap, many schools do find ways of obtaining quantities of off-cuts of softwood suitable for the children to use. Interesting pieces of natural wood and driftwood can be collected and lead to conversations about "length", "thickness" and "shape". Woodwork is an activity which requires careful supervision.

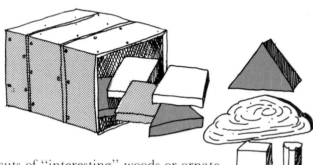

Off-cuts of "interesting" woods or ornate wooden strips for picture frames can be collected and put out to be handled, looked at and talked about.

Example
A box of wood of various shapes and sizes was brought by a father. Paul (3.11) selected two pieces of wood, one longer than the other. He then added a small piece to the shorter piece of wood. "Now they're the same."

The children should be allowed to make things or play with the wood as they wish, but other materials may extend the possibility for experiment. Bags of string, bottle tops, cylinders, etc. can be added to the basic shape—either tacked on with nails or glued on later. Dowels and broom handles are useful.

The length of nails, in relation to the thickness of the wood they are to go through, can be discussed and reasons for the protrusion of nails arrived at.

Example

Robert (4.2): This short nail won't go through this thick piece of wood.
Teacher: What do you need then?
Robert: I need a long nail to go right through.
Teacher: Can you see one?
Robert: This will go through. (Picking up a long nail.)

It is important that the children should be able to play freely in this way, and again although it might be appropriate to talk with them about the materials beforehand or afterwards, if a model has been completed, a great deal can be learnt simply by observation.

Hammers of various sizes, saws, planes and sandpaper blocks can be stored on a clipboard and if outlines of the various tools are drawn on the cupboard, this provides a good matching activity at clearing-up time.

Vocabulary: longer/shorter than – long enough – same length – wide/narrower than – through – inside – next to – on top of.

The teacher's role

Raw materials are the source of much spontaneous interest, experiment and creative play. Mathematical experience may be involved incidentally in many of these activities, but the teacher must decide when it is appropriate to bring it to the surface.

Children need the opportunity to play freely and creatively with raw materials, and concern for mathematical ideas will probably have little place in this kind of activity.

The teacher, however, creates the opportunity for experiment and choice in the provision that she makes. Variety offers opportunity for comparisons and the discovery of new and different properties, which may be generalised later; experience of many rounded things will suggest that "rounded things roll". When the teacher involves the children in the preparation and clearing away of each activity, then further opportunity for sorting and sharing, and experiences of shape and space will occur.

The examples which follow are just some of those opportunities which have occurred in particular circumstances. They do not show how to impose mathematics, but occasions when mathematical experiences and ideas have naturally been involved and sometimes explored, as each teacher has thought appropriate.

Example 1
In this example the teacher has provided a collection of shells for the children to explore. Shirley (4.6) and Trevor (4.8) are looking at the shells and their teacher, noticing their interest in the different kinds, joins with them to initiate a "spontaneous" sorting activity.

Shirley: I've got a tiny one.
Trevor: This is a big one. It's like a stick.
Shirley: Feel this. This is a smooth one.
Trevor: I've got a smooth one.
Shirley: Here's another stick one.
Teacher: Put the stick ones together.
Shirley: And the smooth ones.

The children put the shells in appropriate groups, "stick ones" "tiny ones", "curly ones", "smooth ones". Other children join them.

Shirley: I've got a little tiny one. (Puts it with large shells of the same type, then replaces it with the tiny ones.)
Teacher: Why have you put it there?
Shirley: Because it's tiny. Look at all these. (She presents a collection of mussel shells of all sizes.) Let's put these here.
Trevor: Here's another flat one. Let's put them with the other flat ones.
Teacher: What sort are these? (Holds up a limpet shell.)
Shirley: Shells.
Teacher: But they are all shells. (The children smile.)

Example 2
These children were "painting" the outside wall with water. Their teacher had provided different sized brushes. This is her observation of their activity.

They chose their brushes and were measuring them side by side.

Ceri (4.7):	Mine's bigger—let's measure.
Victoria (4.3):	Mine's too tiny, it won't do anything.
Shelly (4.4):	It's because the point is too small.
Victoria:	The bristles are too small. It will take a long time to cover my wall.
Shelly:	Not mine, because my brush has more water.
Paul (4.8):	You can't reach this high, Ceri.
Ceri:	I can. (Standing on her toes.)
Paul:	Not really, only on your toes. It's too high for you.
Victoria:	(Measuring her height against Ceri.) I'll be able to reach. I'm nearer it.

Examples 3 and 4 show how a teacher has involved several children in the making of two different puppets. In example 4, she involved them in her use of a book for instruction, and asks for their suggestions to solve her "problems". Example 5 shows how she invites the children to suggest the colour to be used and then follows up this interest with a quite spontaneous sorting and comparison.

Example 3

A group was looking at a book showing the various kinds of puppets to be made. One was made using a toilet roll. The teacher held up a rectangular piece of paper.

Teacher:	How can we make this piece into a tube?
Elliott (4.3):	You can roll it around and fasten it. Now you need a face and arms. Draw his face with your pen.
Teacher:	How can we make arms?
Elliott:	You need a long piece to go right round him.

Example 4

Another group of children were helping to make a puppet.

Teacher:	What colour eyes shall we give him?
Joanne (3.1):	Blue. I've got blue.
Russell (4.1):	Brown, because I've got brown.
Teacher:	Shall we see how many children have brown eyes and how many have blue?

The children counted and nine had brown eyes and four had blue eyes.

Teacher:	Are there more children with brown eyes or more with blue eyes?
Marie (4.4):	There are more with brown eyes.
Teacher:	Shall we give our puppet brown eyes, then?

In the next example, Christopher shows some difficulty in solving a practical problem.

Example 5

The teacher stands back and observes Christopher (4.7) as he tries to cut right through a block of wood with a tenon saw only half its width. Knowing Christopher, she has judged it right to leave him to make his own attempts, though had he not succeeded she would probably have joined him and discussed the solution with him.

Christopher was sawing through a piece of wood held in the vice. The saw stuck when it reached its own depth, but he kept on trying. Eventually he removed the wood from the vice, turned it round and sawed until both cuts met.

Example 6   Box Work

The teacher left the children to use the materials provided and observed their activity and invited comment afterwards. There was little or no talking within the group as most were engrossed with making the boxes stick. These children showed most response when they had *finished* modelling and were only interested in talking about their own model—very little interest in those made by others in the group.

Sarah (4.10):   The people are going up into the boat. They're tall. (Pointing with her finger.)

Lisa (4.10):   My boat has big guns and little guns.

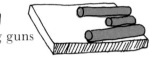

Robert (4.11):   These are binoculars and this is a telescope. They are round.

Craig (5.0):   (Immature.) Mine's a boat. It carries people to the beach.
Teacher: What is this part?
Craig: That's the gun in case someone shoots the people. There are lots of people inside the boat. (Pointing.)

Helen (4.11):   It's a house-boat. There are lots of boxes.

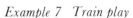

Example 7   Train play
Teacher: I've brought a lot of new boxes from the shop. Would you like to make another train?
Ian (3.11), without answering went to inspect the boxes. He chose a small box and said "This is my coal box." He then selected a similar box saying, "That's the engine." He stood the boxes side by side and then realised that they were the same size. He returned one to the pile and got a larger one.
Teacher: We shall need a cylinder.
Ian: Yes, that's for the chimney.
He chose a very long one and realising it was too long chose a smaller one. The children then started arranging the boxes to make the train. With some assistance they fastened the boxes together. Jill (4.6) wanted the chimney to be in the corner but Ian insisted on the middle and won. The engine box had a centre "handle" and Ian took a long time sighting his chimney by this. Ian taped the bottom of the cylinder only. Jill realised it would need taping near the top as well. "We'll have to tie it there or it will just fall down." The teacher said, "We'll need to find something circular to draw round so we can cut some nice round shapes for our wheels." The children had decided to have cardboard wheels, but they found four wooden circles which they decided would do for wheels. Ian said, "We want two on the engine and two on the coal box." He then found some black crêpe paper and put some in his coal box saying, "There, that is the coal."
Teacher: Can I come for a ride in your train?
Ian: No, you're too big.
Teacher: If you found a bigger box could we add it to the train for me to sit in?
Ian went off and came back with a box the same size as the ones that had been used for the train.
Teacher: Will I be able to get into that box?
Ian: Yes. Put your legs in first and then you just fit in.
Teacher got into the box and with a struggle sat down.
Teacher: I think I'm going to need a much larger box.
Ian: I'll go and get one. (Coming back.) I can't find a large box so you can't come.

Appendix A   Ways with paint

Varying paint

Soap flakes, Polycell, wallpaper paste and sawdust can be used as paint thickeners. Grated crayon added to paint produces interesting effects and can give different shades of colour. The passage of time taken for the paint to thicken might also be discussed.

Just two colours of paint can be used to produce different colours. One colour with white will give different shades of the one colour.

Applying paint

Paint can be applied with: combs, flat lolly sticks, tooth-brushes, foam/wool rollers, feathers, twigs, other natural materials, rolling pins wrapped with string or wool or with cotton reel tracks. It can also be blown with straws or dripped from straws.

Different surfaces to be painted

Perspex	Blackboard	Corrugated card
Aluminium tinfoil	Newspaper	Blotting paper
Formica	Wallpaper	

Attention to shape

Sticky tape applied to plain paper, when peeled off after paint has been applied and dried, leaves a clear outline to shapes.

Wax resist   Shapes can be drawn with wax candles and then painted over—the paint will not be absorbed by the waxed areas.

Paint "splattered" on to cut-out shapes arranged on paper, will produce a silhouette of these shapes when they are removed. Leaves produce a pleasing effect.

Coloured paint or ink dripped from straws onto wet blotting paper will produce radiating patterns.

Symmetry

Paintings may be folded to produce a symmetrical print. It might be interesting to fold the paper in different ways. A wall mirror in the painting area can stimulate the children's attention to natural symmetry.

Finger painting

Finger painting is, of course, a great favourite. Paint may be thickened with paste and larger surfaces like formica table tops used. When the children have had enough of their play, then prints are sometimes made of the finished effect, by gently pressing paper on the paint pattern. The painted area may be compared with its print.

Appendix B   Recipes for play dough

Mix plain flour and water with a little salt. Add *food* colouring.

1 cup salt	2 tablespoons cooking oil
3 cups flour	Food colouring
$\frac{1}{2}$ cup water	

Make up a thickish paste from polycell or other wallpaper paste. Add sawdust until you can knead it.

Avoid paste which contains fungicide, and sawdust from wood treated with preservative.

Some colour powder paints are best avoided; yellow tends to smell, red can stain. The dough should be covered with a cloth after each session to prevent a crust forming, or stored in an airtight container. When left in the air dough will dry out and models harden.

7 Towards Number

Introduction

Number is an abstract idea and many experiences are needed before "three", or "ten", or any other number is understood. No-one, for example, has ever seen a "three"; the symbol 3 is just a shorthand devised by man. The *idea* of three comes as an abstraction from many sets of three objects: although no-one has ever seen three, children can see three cars, three people, three umbrellas, three miscellaneous objects, and so on, and eventually they will understand the "threeness of three".

One of the first ideas towards understanding number is accordingly that of a *set* of objects (cars or people, etc.). Sets are often formed by *sorting*. Things are put together which are in some way alike or belong together. This might be on the basis of a particular attribute such as colour or shape, or a more abstract quality such as use or even "because I like them".

Apart from sorting, many other concepts are needed for the understanding of number, for example that of *one-to-one correspondence*. Young children will pass through a stage when they will believe that row A in the illustration below has the same number as row B because they "look the same"; they apparently take up the same space.

Matching objects *one-to-one* is a technique for checking whether one set has more or fewer objects than another, or the same amount. Only when children can do this confidently can counting have any meaning, as counting is simply matching objects (or people, or whatever is being counted) with numbers.

Another necessary concept is that of *comparison*. Eventually the children will understand, for example, that four is greater than three by comparing a set of four things with a set of three things. Comparison is also a preliminary to *ordering*. As soon as there are more than two things to be compared, they will be ordered according to a particular relationship. Numbers are ordered according to the relation "is greater than", but many other ordering experiences should be provided beforehand.

Yet another concept is that of *invariance* of number of elements in a set. A child may be able to count the five ducks but have to recount if they are moved round to form a different pattern.

This chapter deals with all these concepts "towards number". In the past, because children have been able to chant numbers in order (1, 2, 3 . . .), it has sometimes been assumed that they understood them and so were ready for sums. Time spent in acquiring the preliminary concepts will amply repay itself later in terms of understanding, enjoyment and proficiency in mathematics.

Young children need to experience the ideas through their play. It is practical activity that is important; the handling of a whole range of materials. The help of a skilled adult, who can stand back and observe and who is ready also to join with a child as he plays, to focus his attention and talk with him, is also important.

It would be difficult, and undesirable, to isolate experiences which lead towards an understanding of number, when so many arise naturally out of everyday activities. It is these everyday experiences which help the child towards understanding. The suggestion of some possibilities will undoubtedly recall others to mind.

Some early number books and friezes can be a useful talking point, used by an adult with one or two of the older children. There is a danger, however, that number friezes badly used may lead children to relate for instance, five *only* with five ducks or a domino pattern. As always, variety of experience and talk with the teacher are important. Some books that have proved useful are:

Gretz, Susanna, *Teddy Bears One to Ten*, Armada Picture Lions, Collins, 1973.
Wildsmith, Brian, *The Circus*, Oxford University Press, 1970.
Wildsmith, Brian, *1 2 3*, Oxford University Press, 1965.
Peppe, Rodney, *Circus Numbers*, Longmans, 1969.
Oxenbury, Helen, *Numbers of things*, Heinemann, 1967.

Jan Pienkowski's friezes, *1 2 3 Frieze* and *Shape Frieze*, published by Gallery Five, have also proved useful.

Possible developments

Sorting

Sorting, putting together those things that are alike or belong together, is a natural reaction for many children when playing with a collection of objects. Before this sorting can take place, however, each object must be classified. The identity and classification a child chooses may not be ones which are obvious to an adult observer, and may not even be ones which the child himself is able to verbalise.

It is important that young children should have the opportunity to handle and play freely with a whole range of materials. These experiences will help them to become familiar with all kinds of things, from shells and pebbles to bricks and plastic shapes. Classifying arises from an ability to observe similarities and differences. A skilled adult can encourage children to make comparisons and talk with them to help them to identify differences that they can see but cannot label with a word.

This sort of discussion might be prompted by a child's chance remark, "Look, I've got one like that"—a judgement which might be explored—"Yes, it does look like that one, but is it exactly the same?" Alternatively, the teacher may take the initiative: "Can you find one that looks the same as this one? Is it the same or is there something different about it?"

It might be easier to use a few objects with clearly differentiated attributes as a starting point, but conversations of this kind can occur spontaneously in many activities. Colour and shape have always been used as a basis for sorting, but objects may have many properties, and can be sorted, for example, according to size, weight or texture.

At adult level, for instance, a collection of objects identified as lorry, car, car and bicycle, might be sorted in many different ways. They might be sorted by their identity into lorry, cars and bicycle, according to a particular attribute (colour, shape, weight, size, texture, etc.),

things that are green   things that are not green

by some group identity (in this case modes of transport), or some more abstract quality.

things that are   things that are
driven by an engine   not driven by an engine

They might be sorted according to any combination of these, such as things which are "green and made of metal", but such sophisticated sorting is seldom within the range of the very young child. Young children will be exploring the identity and simple attributes of objects that they can see and feel.

Sorting is not, of course, restricted to the use of "sorting toys". Children often find endless pleasure in sorting and re-sorting boxes of buttons, odd pieces of materials, pebbles, a "lost pieces" tray and other inexpensive collections. Many everyday activities involve incidental sorting. Though it takes time and a great deal of adult help at first, young children can take an active role in caring for equipment and tidying it away. Puzzles and games must be sorted into the right boxes, boxes placed in cupboards, books on shelves and blocks packed away.

There are times when the teacher might impose restrictions by asking, for example, for "all the blue balls to be put into the basket", or, "all those wearing red to fetch their coats", or she might ask the children to sort a collection into just two piles. It is also useful to give the occasional "negative" instruction: "All those *not* wearing red fetch their coats".

Provision and guidance are at the discretion of the sensitive adult. Some activities which might involve experience of sorting are discussed below:

Making collections of all kinds
For example: junk materials; flowers; shells; natural objects; leaves; marbles; scraps of material; buttons; bottletops.

Making collections for display
The items can be gathered by children themselves, for example, shiny things; things of a particular colour; things of a particular texture (rough, smooth, prickly); particular shapes (rounded, with holes, pointed, with straight sides, spirals, etc.); things we use in the kitchen or bathroom; things that we use to draw with or cook with.

Tidying up
The teacher could provide containers (boxes, drawers, jars, etc.), perhaps labelled with colour pictures, so that equipment can be sorted and put in the right place. Ask the children to replace things that belong in each area (Home Corner, shop, water tray, etc.).

Containers, drawers and shelves could be provided in the Home Corner, shop, etc., so that articles can be sorted and put away.

Sorting of apparatus, bought or improvised
Farm and animals   Field markings, hedges and buildings can provide boundaries to contain different kinds of animals.

Animals, birds, people, vehicles   These can all extend the range of sorting.

House, furniture, people   Doll's house furniture may be sorted to be placed in particular rooms.

Junk material   Children might like to make rooms and furniture for themselves out of junk material.

Garage, cars, lorries, etc.   Vehicles might be grouped according to colour, use, whether "broken down", number of wheels, etc.

Picture cards   These might be classified and sorted according to those that look alike, those that are of a particular colour or design, etc.

Logiblocks (attribute blocks).

Plastic shapes   Many kinds are available. Provision of coloured hoops or trays may prompt sorting especially by colour.

Making sets of themselves
Sometimes children will themselves become part of a set—children wearing red, sandals, hair ribbon, etc.; children sitting on the mat, floor, grass, etc.

Vocabulary: looks like – looks different – same – all – belongs together – put together – inside – (and words which identify, describe and compare objects).

One-to-one correspondence

Young children are very much influenced by "the way things look" rather than the way they are.

Example
The children were looking at a picture showing two rows of cats.

Teacher:	Are there more fat cats than thin cats?
David (3.7):	No.
Nicholas (3.10):	No, they take the same room.
Teacher:	Are there more thin ones?
Alistair (3.7):	No. There are the same number.

Placing things in one-to-one correspondence enables children to make a visual check of whether there are, in fact, "more", "fewer" or "the same".

There are many incidental opportunities for children to need to put objects in one-to-one correspondence. Some examples of one-to-one correspondence which arise in particular activities are given below.

Tidying up
Hanging hats on hooks, wigs on stands, and coats on pegs —perhaps with picture symbols.

Replacing pencils and scissors in spaces in a rack.

Hanging equipment on hooks and pegs, where there is one hook or peg for each piece of equipment to be stored in this way—perhaps labelled with a picture symbol.

Replacing lids on boxes and jars.

Returning trays or drawers into appropriate spaces.

In Home Corner areas, replacing lids, using cups with saucers or hanging them on hooks provided.

Growing things
Planting one bulb in each pot.
Separating seeds, plants; perhaps each one replanted in its own section of an egg box.

Themselves
Finding a "partner" or "friend"—perhaps to use the seesaw.
Buttoning a coat (often easier to button a friend's!).

Meal times
There might be one cloth for each table; one place mat for each setting; one napkin, mug, knife, fork and spoon for each setting; one plate and one chair for each child.

Baking
Providing an apron for each child.

Putting a helping of mixture into each tray or cake case.

Making one cake for each child in the group, or the class. Topping the cakes; perhaps with one cherry each.

Milk
There should be one straw to be put into each bottle; either each child does his own or one child takes a turn for the group.

The children should take one bottle each, or the milk should be distributed one-to-one by a "monitor".

Sometimes children place a symbol or name tag on a bottle at the beginning of the day to label their own. Some exchange a symbol or name card for a bottle at milk time.

The bottles must be placed in the crate. Are there enough spaces?

Sometimes children must wait for an empty chair at the milk table before they can sit down.

Block play
Building two towers with similar sized bricks, matching one-to-one to build towers of similar height. Perhaps copying a tower already made.

Building towers of different sized bricks but using bricks in one-to-one correspondence, probably with the teacher's guidance.

Other apparatus
Placing objects in one-to-one correspondence according to texture in "feely puzzle".

Fitting lids to different-sized jars.

Matching pairs of cards; there are many different sets of cards produced for this purpose.

Vocabulary: one each – enough – as many as – pair.

Comparisons of number

Once a child is able to match one-to-one with confidence, he can use the idea to make a visual comparison of the number of objects contained in two sets. In this way the child can make the comparisons "more than" or "fewer than" or "same as".

A young child faced with a row of cups and a pile of saucers might have no other way of finding whether he has enough saucers to put with the cups than to match them as far as possible, one-to-one. In this way he can check whether there are "more", "fewer" or "the same" cups as saucers, without using number.

Making comparisons between two sets also enables the child to establish a relationship between them, and is one step towards the later understanding of the relationship "is greater than" or "is less than" between two numbers.

Children often attract our attention when they think that someone has "more" than they do. A spontaneous remark can often be followed up by a simple check. A child who thinks his friend has more blocks can be helped to compare his set of blocks with that of his friend by placing each of his blocks in correspondence with one of those of his friend. Those blocks which have no "partner" will indicate who has "more" and, of course, who has "fewer".

There may be a case for sometimes deliberately providing "too many" or "too few" of, for example, straws for bottles, to enable children to verbalise what they, in some cases, intuitively see.

Some examples of situations in which comparison of number may be necessary are given below.

Taking turns
In many activities each child will need to have a piece of equipment to use for himself—a bike, a chair, a place setting at meal-time, a piece of paper, and so on. Children will soon discover if there are "fewer" bikes, chairs, etc. than children wanting to use them.

Meal-times

Children involved in preparing for meal-times will need to put out one mug for each child and may rely on one-to-one correspondence without counting.

A child putting a straw into each of the bottles in the crate will not know whether he has enough straws for bottles until he has distributed them one-to-one. Similarly a plate of biscuits may not contain enough for "one each" and children would not know until each had taken one or they had run out.

Baking

Children making sandwich biscuits might be allocated "tops" or "bottoms". They will need to check whether they have made the same amount of each and if they are not able to count, then they can correspond one-to-one "tops" with "bottoms".

Vocabulary: enough – not enough – more than – fewer than – too many – same as.

Ordering

Any comparison of more than two objects will involve "ordering" them according to the chosen criterion. If we compare the height of A, B, and C, shown below, we

A B C

can see that B is at the same time linked with A, which it follows and C that it precedes, and the three are ordered in sequence: A, B, C. B is, at the same time, taller than A and shorter than C.

Numbers are ordered according to the relationship "is greater than", but before children begin to use numbers and understand the basis of their order, they will encounter the notion of ordering in many other ways, based on the kind of comparisons that were mentioned in the section on sorting, such as length, weight, height and width.

Ordering of this kind will probably occur in the arrangement of goods in the "shop", or books and boxes on the class shelves, or play with different sized dolls and clothes. Stories like "The Three Bears" or "The Three Billy Goats Gruff", which involve ordering, can be good starting points, developed in creative work, and used as a basis for talk with the children.

It may be that some young children will achieve a stage where they are ready to compare more than two sets to see which has "most" or "least", but incidental experience of this kind is less frequent.

saucers   spoons

cups

Using number names and counting

Many of the rhymes and stories which we use with young children include the use of number names. (See chapter 12

Rhymes and Stories.) Children often become familiar with the number names long before they achieve any understanding of their meaning. It is not unusual for children to recite happily from one to ten in a number rhyme or as they play, but the teacher does not assume that they can therefore use number or count.

Counting attaches a different verbal number symbol to a set of units as one unit is added. In effect we are saying:

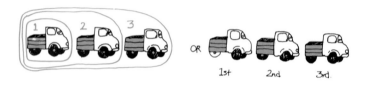

as each object is moved to join the previous one.

Young children need a lot of experience of touching and counting, with an adult to listen and help if necessary. From a distance it is easy to believe that a child is counting when in fact he is only reciting a number sequence and touching or moving objects at random. Children have to learn that it is easier to start at one end of a line of objects and finish at the other. Counting objects placed anyhow or counting, for example, beads on a ring, or cakes in a patty-tin, the child must learn to establish a starting and ending point of his own. Scatter counting is a fairly sophisticated skill for young children, and they will need lots of help and practice.

Invariance

It is not obvious to the very young child that a set of objects has the same number of units however those units are arranged (provided, of course, that none are removed or added).

At this stage, however, we can offer many opportunities for children to arrange and re-arrange the objects in a set and see whether they need to re-count each time. Although some children may be capable of finding there are the same number of things in two sets (by matching), they may not be at all sure there are still the same number of the objects if one of the sets is differently arranged.

Informal fractions

Informal fractions, especially "half", are frequently used as approximate measures in incidental discussion. Cutting into "four" or "three" tends to be talked about rather than "quarters" or "thirds", although fractions are sometimes used.

Problems of sharing arise at meal-times, during baking and when sharing materials.

Numerals

Children come across written numbers, just as they come across written words, long before they are able to read or understand them. Until a child has achieved that understanding, a numeral is just a shape with no real meaning.

Example
Paula (4.5) was painting.
Paula: I made a letter.
Teacher: That's a number. That's number four.
Paula: I made a four. What's a letter? Make me a letter.
Teacher: I'll make a letter P for Paula. Like this.
Paula copied the shape and said, "I made a four and a P".

The teacher's role

The teacher is the initiator of many of the activities which lead towards number. In many cases it is she who develops an opportunity for talk with the children, following their interest in the activities provided, and pursues attention to ideas like one-to-one correspondence, comparison and so on. Children need the variety of experience and the attention to detail that the teacher is able to encourage.

In this first example we see how a teacher is able to initiate a sorting activity following a child's chance remark. Her presence and interest doubtless affect the children's attention to similarity and difference.

Example 1
The children were playing with a mass of junk boxes, all shapes and sizes.

Tania (5.2):   Look how many I've got.
Mark (4.10):   What a mess on the table.
Teacher: Let's sort them out—are there any the same?

The children soon got the idea and sorted things of similar size and shape, e.g. egg boxes and yoghurt pots. Some noticed that the cereal packets were wider or longer than soap packets. When they had grouped things into general sets, they began to subdivide them, e.g. different types of egg boxes, different pictures on yoghurt pots, different coloured polystyrene trays, long tubes and short tubes. They noted two Bisto packets, that had the same picture, were different sizes. Afterwards they fitted everything into a big box.

In this second example a teacher observes the child's confusion over the invariance of number.

Example 2
Jonathan (3.4) was trying to fit a milk bottle into a crate with no spaces. He took one bottle out to put his own in, took another one out to put a second one in, and this proceeded up the line and down the next until he realised he was always left with one in hand. He then took two bottles out with the same result. He did this a few times before he realised the result would always be the same. Finally he took a whole lot of bottles out in the hope that in the ensuing muddle they would all finally be fitted in.

Example 3
Is this child really ready to count? Could she not use one-to-one correspondence to check?

Tara (4.6):   (Looked at two towers of bricks—each six bricks high—counted . . .) One, two, three, four, seven, five, six.
Teacher: And how many here?
Tara: One, two, three, six, seven, eight.
Teacher: How many?
Tara: Seven.
Teacher: Is there the same number in each tower?
Tara: Yes.
Teacher: Which is bigger?
Tara: Both the same. Yours is bigger.
Teacher: What if we lay them down?
Tara: Now mine's little and yours is little too.

8 Apparatus, Toys and Games

Introduction

Children learn by *doing*. It is therefore not surprising that the provision of apparatus (both large and small), toys and games, has been accepted as a necessity.

The use of apparatus and toys does not always provide a specific end product, but the experiences of building, matching, sharing, comparing and taking apart can all lead towards mathematical concepts. Many of the matching, sorting and ordering activities can arise incidentally within the periods of tidying away and clearing up. It is not always the child who has been building that does the packing away. Some children really enjoy helping to fill a box or shelves in the correct way.

Example
Toby (4.5) had been playing with blocks, but then wandered away and the blocks were put away by two other boys, who spent a long time carefully fitting the different sizes of blocks into the two boxes. With only a few left to pick up Jo (4.1) said, "We've nearly put them all away."

Both Toby and Jo had valuable experiences, although the more obvious mathematical one may be said to lie with Jo and his companion in their appreciation of the relative sizes of the blocks and their places in the storage boxes.

Although some material with particular mathematical structure will be mentioned, it is sometimes restrictive in the overall experience it provides for very young children by the very nature of its structure. Therefore it is often preferable to select materials that do not have such a tight-knit structure; when appropriate, the teacher can extend the enquiries and discoveries with these along the lines of the structured material.

Large apparatus to climb into/out of/through/under/over, and push/pull toys of various sizes may help to give the children ideas of weight, speed, height, width and length, while increasing their spatial awareness. Other mathematical experiences with large apparatus are discussed more fully in chapters 9 and 10 *Outdoor Activities* and *The Environment*.

Constructional kits, jigsaws, inset boards and stacking or nesting toys provide practice in fitting, ordering and estimating shapes and sizes.

Games may be of the type where at the conclusion there is a specific winner, but for very young children the games are generally more in the form of an activity to experience and complete on an individual basis. The emphasis is on personal achievement.

Ideas leading towards mathematical concepts can be gained from all the toys and apparatus.

The next section will indicate the value of a teacher's comment or direct intervention is at the relevant time within the activity. But on many occasions children gain mathematical experience without any intervention by an adult.

Possible developments

Building blocks

Whenever a place is being furnished for the use of young children, a set of blocks is generally considered one of the basic pieces of equipment to be provided. A glance through the catalogues soon brings the realisation that the choice is much greater than existed even a few years ago. Expense considerations aside, there is much variety in size, material, weight (whether solid or hollow), colour and texture. Ideally, provision should be made to cover all these factors but the important thing is to have plenty in each set. If expense must be curtailed, then it is probably better to have a plentiful supply (at least 100) of two or three sorts rather than a small quantity of many; it can be exasperating to have insufficient blocks of a kind to complete a construction.

As well as wooden blocks, there are now many kinds of plastic and PVC-coated foam blocks on the market. These have a slightly wider range of shapes and are often much bigger than their wooden counterparts but much lighter. The surfaces seem to impart slight "stiction" to the blocks when stacked together.

Young children often play with just one block at a time; they may stand on it, sit on it and use it in their imaginative play as a parcel, steering wheel or tool. Then, as they discover more blocks and those of various shapes and sizes, building begins.

The addition of such accessories as steering wheels, steps

and hosepipes can encourage imaginative play where spatial ideas such as inside, outside, on top of and underneath are likely to be explored. Hollow blocks of various sizes and types involve even more ideas of space, volume and area, for example, they can be used as windows or garages.

When children play with toy animals, cars, lorries, etc. in conjunction with blocks, there may also be opportunities for sorting and making comparisons.

Tower building

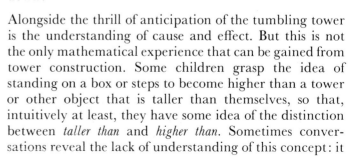

Many children start block play by building upwards to make a tower. The principal aim seems to be to find out how far it can be extended. The towers collapse when the height becomes too great and the vocabulary arising from this activity is usually of the type, "Can I make it fall down?"

Alongside the thrill of anticipation of the tumbling tower is the understanding of cause and effect. But this is not the only mathematical experience that can be gained from tower construction. Some children grasp the idea of standing on a box or steps to become higher than a tower or other object that is taller than themselves, so that, intuitively at least, they have some idea of the distinction between *taller than* and *higher than*. Sometimes conversations reveal the lack of understanding of this concept: it has still to be formed in the minds of some of the children.

Through tower building there is a development of vocabulary from the original *big* and *small* to more selective comparatives.

Example

Alistair (3.4):	Mine is taller.
Wayne (4.2):	Mine is big as well.
Alistair:	So is mine.
Wayne:	Put yours on top of mine then we'll have a giant one!

Example

Matthew (3.10) and Claire (3.6) are trying to make a tower the size of Claire.

Claire:	We need some more bricks, I reckon.
Matthew:	We must put some more of those on.
Claire:	It is too tall—now take some off.
Matthew:	That is just the right size now.

Alistair and Wayne show they have appreciated that the addition of one tower to the other will create a new tower that is taller than either of its component towers, whereas Matthew and Claire have been looking at the inverse operation—one brick less and the tower is lower.

Taking one of a pair of identical towers and re-building in another form, e.g.

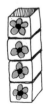

helps the child towards the idea of invariance of number—there are the same number of blocks "before" and "after" although they look different.

Example

Helen (3.10) had built two towers of blocks, each containing the same number of blocks of equal size.

Helen:	Look, that one's the biggest and that's the smallest.

Khusam (4.7) had also built two tall towers of similar height.

Khusam:	They are the same. One is bigger and one is bigger.

Apparently Helen and Khusam are both experiencing difficulty with "the same height" in relation to the biggest and the smallest. But although the symptoms may appear to be similar, for Helen it is a lack of the concept of equality whereas Khusam is lost for the appropriate vocabulary.

Building on a flat surface

An alternative start to block play is to build along a flat surface either in a line like a roadway or as a tabloid.

 "Tabloid"    "Roadway"

In these instances the problems of balance are avoided and the emphasis becomes an awareness of matching the blocks in some way, and the need to encourage the development of relevant vocabulary is all the more pressing.

Example

A group of children were making a road with blocks.

Lorraine (4.5):	It's getting too long. We'll have to make a roundabout.

Many sets of blocks consist only of regular shapes. The addition of off-cuts of wood, trimmed and made splinter-proof, with irregular shapes, can make the materials much more stimulating.

Obvious discussion points are based on the introduction of the mathematical names for the more common shapes and of some of their properties, but only in the simplest terms, e.g. which shapes will roll, which will slide, etc. and these discussions can be centred at one time upon the three-dimensional solid and on another occasion on the two-dimensional bounding surfaces.

Solids have faces which meet at edges which, in turn, meet at corners. How many faces? Draw a different pattern on each one. How many patterns have you drawn?

Interlocking bricks
With interlocking bricks it is possible to go further away from the plumb than with smooth blocks (wood, cork, etc.), but there is a limit to how far such non-alignment can go. One teacher commented on the "bent" tower a child had made through careless and partial use of an interlocking system. Once his attention was drawn to the bending, the child dismantled the tower but before he could rebuild it properly, the teacher challenged him to build another bent tower. Now his attention was focussed on why the tower had bent and his second effort not only bent as before but was even taller than the previous tower. Just to satisfy herself that he understood how it was he was able to build out of the vertical, the teacher asked if he could make a bent tower with wooden building blocks.

The structures below made by Aaron (4.5) demonstrate an extension of the experience which interlocking bricks provide.

A man walking (the small bricks are staggered)

A see-saw (small bricks placed centrally)

The first two "models" could be created with wooden blocks of the conventional type, but not the slide.

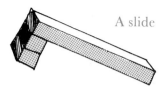

A slide

Vocabulary: heavy – heavier – light – lighter – long – longer – high – higher – low – lower – short – shorter – up – down – tall – taller – more – less – side – edge – corner – face.

Constructional kits

Blocks and connector rods
Some structures merely seem to satisfy an urge to build but not any desire to simulate an existing object or building. There is often a sense of balance, or equivalence, within the construction and many are quite complex.

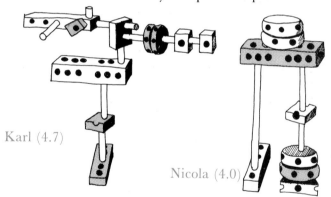

Karl (4.7)

Nicola (4.0)

Much of the experience given by these constructional toys is concerned with size, shape and linear dimensions, but the next example is an instance involving balance and weight.

Example
Patrick (4.8) made a "tree" with the blocks and connector rods. The addition of a new "branch" caused the tree to

fall. The teacher talked with him about balance and he was able to tell her that one stick was heavier because it was longer. He went on to experiment with how far a branch could be extended in any one direction before the tree tipped over.

A week later, Tracey (4.5) made an umbrella from junk materials (a large egg carton and a toilet roll tube). She did not have the tube central and the umbrella would not balance. The teacher referred her back to the work done with connector rods and scales and then asked her what she needed to do. "Make the sides the same", Tracey replied, and on being asked "How?" she moved the tube to a more central position relative to the box.

A further four days had elapsed and both Patrick and Tracey were playing with the connector rods. Patrick was again experimenting with balance, deliberately trying to build a construction that would over-balance (a word given to him by the teacher during their earlier discussions). Tracey made a tree with an equal number of rods protruding from each side and all of the same size. In spite of this, the tree would not stand up, yet when asked if she thought her tree was balanced she said, "Yes".

When Patrick was asked if he thought it was balanced, he replied "No, because it keeps over-balancing". When asked why he thought this was so, without examining the tree he said, "It cannot be the same on both sides". The teacher responded, "It looks the same to me—do you think both sides are the same?" Tracey said, "Yes, they are". Patrick now inspected it closely and said, "One must be heavier than the other or it wouldn't fall down". Later, Patrick discovered that Tracey's tree would not balance as one rod was not pushed in as far as the others.

Tracey had been dominated by the perceptual aspects and had equated balance with apparent symmetry. Patrick went on to build irregular, non-symmetrical shapes with

the connector rods that maintained perfect balance.

This was not a one-off experience but rather the culmination of many experiments, much discussion and thoughtful provision of leading ideas by the teacher.

Figure Craft
Figure Craft and similar types of material usually stimulate the child to make figures where choice of size, shape and colour play their part. To make them stand up without toppling over needs an understanding of balance, and vocabulary related to over-balancing, top-heavy, etc. can be introduced.

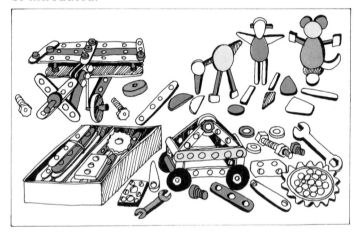

Equipment such as *Fit-Bits*, *Plastic Meccano*, *Junior Engineer* and *Bilofix*, requires the manipulative skills of fitting nuts on to bolts. In fastening the strips together to construct any model, choice has to be made of the correct size of nut and bolt involving both sorting, matching and then screwing. Similarly, choice of the appropriate parts to bolt together must be made if a child is copying a model from the drawings usually supplied with a kit (involving size, shape and matching). If, however, there is no attempt to copy a pattern, there is often more appreciation of shape in whatever is made—like the four-year-old who made a triangular shape from three strips and correctly named it, whilst another boy (3.9) named the second shape (a square) when he added a fourth strip to the original three.

Sticklebricks give rise to as many types of play and conversation as the interlocking small bricks, but due to their change in physical appearance and the wheel shapes that come in the packs there is a wider provision for imaginative construction. For example, one boy (4.1) made "an air grass cutter with a steering wheel".

Construct-o-Straws or *Orbit* material encourage children to build shapes in three dimensions. On using the straws they often note and comment on the matchings they have made for colour and/or size.

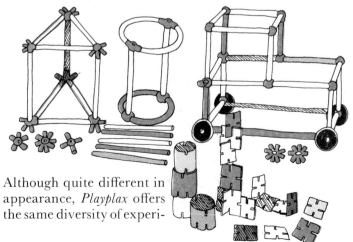

Although quite different in appearance, *Playplax* offers the same diversity of experi-

ience—creative construction involving a sense of balance and pattern or symmetry together with the opportunity to sort according to colour and shape.

Example

Jill (4.9) was using both rings and squares from the kit, saying, "I'm building lots of castles with these".

Teacher: Can you tell me anything about these castles then?

Jill: Well, I made them all with four of those things on one of those round things.

Teacher: You mean the squares.

Jill: Yes, and they are all the same colour.

Vocabulary: high – low – short – shorter – higher – lower – into – out of – balance – centre – ring – square – circle – cube – cylinder.

Structured mathematical apparatus

Some apparatus has a definite mathematical structure, e.g. *Poleidoblocs, Stern apparatus* and *Unifix*. They can be used purely as play material and indeed that is the way to introduce them to children so that each individual child becomes familiar with the parts of the apparatus and the relationships between the parts. Superficially, Poleidoblocs G may be confused with any other set of coloured and polished wooden blocks of various shapes and sizes, but closer inspection will reveal the interlinking relations between many of the blocks. Questions can be asked of a child of the type:

Can you find another block to match this red one?
Can you find a cylinder that is taller than this one?
How many blue cubes do you need to build a cube the same size as the red cube?

Appreciation of the ways in which the various shapes are related enables the teacher to ask further leading questions when a suitable opening presents itself in a child's play (e.g. commenting on the way the flat slabs will go together to make a staircase of three steps—"What would we need to make the next step?").

Other apparatus which is mathematically structured is the set of "logic" or "attribute" blocks. The majority of

suppliers use plastic shapes although the original Dienes floor set was a collection of wooden shapes. In practically every case the collection varies in shape, colour, size and thickness, and there is, consequently, a wide variety of the methods of sorting and matching that can be performed.

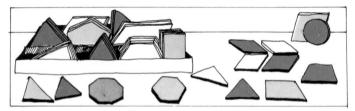

It should be remembered, however, that to describe squares, for example, as thick or thin is not mathematically accurate and if possible, young children should not be confused in this way.

The initial experience for any child is just to play with the pieces to familiarise himself with them all and this often takes the form of picture and pattern making—similar to the early use of the other structured apparatus.

Example

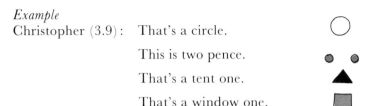

Christopher (3.9) :   That's a circle.

This is two pence.

That's a tent one.

That's a window one.

That's a big cloud up in the sky.

Zoe (4.0) made a symmetrical pattern:

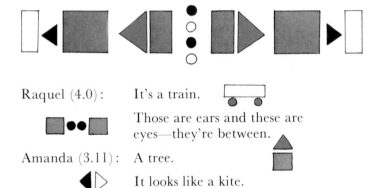

Raquel (4.0) :   It's a train.

Those are ears and these are eyes—they're between.

Amanda (3.11) :   A tree.

It looks like a kite.

Vocabulary: taller than – shorter than – long – longer than – longest – next to – after – before – above – below.

Other apparatus and equipment

Sorting

There are many varieties of wooden and plastic toys meant for counting and sorting. Children often play with them as representational toys (despite their different scales which make comparisons difficult). They use them as stamps or cutters with dough and clay, but in conception they were intended for sorting and matching and thereby to link in with games and toys.

Example

Donna (5.1) and Sharon (4.10) were playing with the Allsorts and had made sets with them placing the sets in columns. When they had sorted the collection completely, they stacked each set in piles.

On another occasion Joanne (4.6) used the Allsorts to sort out into rows.

Even with a collection of beads there can be a similar sorting experience when they are of varied size, shape, colour and texture.

Example

Matthew (4.7): These beads are cylinders and they've got a hole right through them. Those are called cubes and they've got a hole as well.

Patterns and sequences

When children are encouraged to thread beads on a lace to match a particular pattern and then repeat it to the end of the lace, there is development of the idea of sequence. There is as well experience of identification of assorted beads according to shape, size and colour and (maybe) material—wood or plastic. There is often considerable vocabulary used amongst a group of children engrossed in their threading activities which incorporates ideas of growth in length as well as naming colours and shapes of individual beads. The ideas can be consolidated when the teacher is shown the full lace with its pattern of beads (with or without errors in repeat).

Example

Viki (4.3), Sarah (4.8) and Simon (4.6) were tidying drawers containing beads, with the teacher.

Simon: This drawer has big beads and little beads. The little ones don't belong—they go in there.

Sarah: I'm fixing mine into rows—some have holes and some have flat. It looks like a carpet.

Viki: Mine go in rows. This is the yellow row. It looks like a carpet. It has patterns. It's like mummy bear and baby bear. [She had cylindrical beads and meant that each bead had two circles.]

Sarah: But where is daddy bear? I know, you be daddy (to Viki) 'cos yours are biggest. You be mummy (to Simon) and I'll be baby because mine are the smallest.

Viki: This box isn't big enough. There are too many to go in. (Long pause.) I'll make them into double deckers.

Simon: What's that?

Viki: It's one on top of that one. It's two, in a pile—like this.

Patterns and sequences also arise with pegs and a peg-board.

Example

Dawn (4.8) made a symmetrical pattern of squares with pegs, then filled in the rest of the board, working across and down, always putting in a peg next to one already there but the colours were haphazard.

Ian (4.11) filled in evenly in rows from the top, using all yellow pegs for the first two rows then haphazardly using the remaining colours for the rest of the rows. A week later Ian filled in a peg board starting at the outside (perimeter) and making smaller and smaller squares.

Discoveries of shape may also be made with a peg-board, such as, that half a square, divided diagonally, is a triangle, but when the square is divided from the mid-point of one side to the mid-point of the opposite side, it yields two rectangles.

Vocabulary: sort – match – next to – after – before – on top of – underneath – half – quarter.

Toys

In all the equipment mentioned so far, there seems to have been some kind of mathematical experience inherent. But what about the other toys that are to be found in the classroom? Very often it is not the toy by itself that will provide a mathematical experience but rather the way in which it is being used either on its own or in conjunction with other things.

Push and pull toys

Example
Carole (3.11) was manoeuvering a pram up a steep slope. She approached the slope pushing a doll's pram full of dolls and blankets. Finding she couldn't push the pram up the slope, she thought for a few seconds and then tried to pull it up. As this was also unsuccessful, she thought again and then emptied the pram of its contents. Then, with a struggle, she pulled the pram up the slope.

On many occasions a small group of children will be playing with cars, either running them down an incline (a plank resting on a block) or pushing them up. Such activities may spontaneously develop ideas of the degree of push needed to get a car up a slope with cries of, "Push harder—that was too gentle!" The children will soon realise that the steeper the slope the greater the effort required. If the spontaneity is not there, then a word from the teacher may be all that is required.

Another occasion may yield the realisation that the steeper the slope the faster a vehicle will run down it. If the speed is too great then the vehicle may fall off the sides of the plank and crash.

Tracks
Railway lines, with stations, signal boxes, tunnels, bridges, and long or short trains lead to more ideas of spatial awareness. A large enough space on the floor must be found, or the track must wind between the legs of tables and chairs.

Tunnels and bridges must be high enough for the train to go under.

Ramps must be fitted correctly so that the train can run smoothly.

Example
James (3.4) and David (4.2) were constructing a railway track from long pieces of wood supported on blocks. David overlapped his section and the train had to bump over it. James—though younger—butted his pieces of wood so that the train ran smoothly over the joins.

There may be a beginning and end to the track, and the train will go backwards and forwards, instead of round a continuous track.

The engine may be reversed or used to push the trucks

instead of pulling them. There is bound to be conversation about direction.

Cars and lorries of all sizes are often used in the same way, with roadways, intersections, bridges and unloading bays made from blocks or other materials. Less ambitiously, simple networks can be chalked on to the playground.

Buildings

Dolls' houses, bungalows, house and roof units, farm houses, barns, garages, shops and airports all lead to imaginative play, which in turn leads towards ideas of sorting, matching and estimation of size.

> Can you put all the bedroom furniture upstairs in the doll's house?
>
> Put the farmer and his wife in the farmhouse, and what shall we put in the barn?
>
> If that car is too long to go in that garage, try to find a smaller one.

Stacking and nesting

Ideas of comparison and ordering come from playing with the many toys with graded components, e.g. Russian nesting dolls, pyramid rings, stacking cubes and boxes.

Recognition and estimation of size and shape is experienced with posting boxes, hammer toys, ring toys and inset boards.

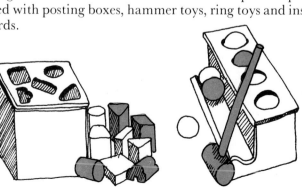

Jigsaw puzzles

Young children nearly always put puzzles together by trial and error, "trying out" each piece against another until it fits. Then, from doing the same puzzle a number of times they remember where each piece fits. Even inset boards, where a child has to match a certain shape, e.g. a lorry to its silhouette, are difficult for the beginner who doesn't always realise that he is trying to put it in upside-down. This shows that he is not really aware of the shape relationship at all, but just remembers or "has a feeling" that it ought to go there.

Example

Andrew (4.8) demonstrates this memory way of doing puzzles.

Teacher:	You can do the puzzle very quickly and it is quite a hard one. Where do you put this piece?
Andrew:	It is the slide and it goes there. I know where they all go.
Teacher:	How do you know?
Andrew:	Because I've done it before.

Joanne (4.4) on the other hand, looks at the shape of pieces.

Example

Teacher:	Do you look at the piece before you put it in?
Joanne:	Yes.
Teacher:	How can you see that it goes there?
Joanne:	Because it's the shape. Because it fits there.

Ian (4.9) has reached a different stage of recognising shapes.

Example

Teacher: What do you do now, if it does not fit?
Ian: I turn it round and try it the other way.

Conversation with adults may lead children towards sorting out straight edges or corners, and with the large floor puzzles it is often possible to match pieces by colour or pattern.

Vocabulary: up – down – slow – fast – higher – lower – backwards – forwards – over – under – above – below – edge – corner – straight – curved.

Games—matching and sorting

Dominoes may be used for matching, as in the game of dominoes itself, and the dots would be seen as patterns to match (not necessarily to count). There are also many types of picture dominoes (animals, fruit, vegetables, colours, shapes, people) all giving practice in matching.

This practice of matching one picture or pattern to another identical one is also given in the game of Lotto and in playing pairing games such as Snap.

Example

The children were playing at the Lotto table.

John (4.6):   Timothy has taken all the cards.
Nicholas (5.0):   Hasn't he to share them out?
Teacher: It would be better to share, wouldn't it, Timothy?
Timothy (4.6):   I have shared. (Pointing to two cards.)
He eventually shared them all out.

The equality of shares is not immediately apparent to young children and experiences to stress this need to be provided. Portioning apples and oranges, handing round a plate of biscuits, etc., are practical ways of giving this experience in an everyday situation.

When playing with Dominoes, Lotto cards, Snap cards, etc., the predominant thought has been to use the pictures or patterns on them for matching one-to-one, yet the example quoted shows valuable spin-offs that lead to other equally important mathematical experiences.

Within sets of pictures and patterns to match, it is often possible to develop games where the matching is not merely one-to-one but a complete set of a kind is collected instead, e.g. Happy Families.

Much of the equipment that is presented as pre-reading material is in fact using these ideas of matching, pairing and visual discrimination, which are equally necessary in the foundation experiences for mathematics.

Many of the games suggested can be applied to sorting toys with suitable adaptation. For example, one animal could be removed from a collection while the children close their eyes. They could then try to find out which one was missing.

One teacher organised a sorting game by asking each child in the group to choose and bring a toy from around the room; there was a farm lorry, a helicopter, a golliwog, a breakdown lorry, a helmet and a domino brick. One child was chosen to sort these toys into two sets while the other children tried to guess her reason. The first time it was "some yellow/no yellow". Then another child sorted them in a different way. This involved the whole group in seeing differences and matching similarities.

Vocabulary: share – match – different – some – all – up – down – inside – outside – under – over – backwards – forwards – sideways – next to.

The teacher's role

There are many important points for a teacher to think about when she prepares a room with toys and other apparatus. She should ask herself questions such as:

How do I decide which to present?
Do I allow every child to choose?
Do I impose my wishes?
Do I allow a change of apparatus or toy at will?
Do I withdraw apparatus when interest in it wanes?
Do I replace it with something else?
Do I sometimes try to link it with similar materials, providing for experience of solving similar problems?

By listening, a teacher will realise that children "talk" a great deal of mathematics while they are playing, and she can find out quite a lot about their stages of development. In this way she can judge when some children are ready to join a group game, enabling her to present them with some small problem that will help to lead them one step further in their mathematical thinking.

Example 1
This teacher was playing with a group of four-year-old children using *Sticklebricks*.

Matthew: I like this colour [yellow] and this colour is for Liverpool [red].
Jason: Let's find all the reds. I'll find the most.
All the *Sticklebricks* were piled to one side.
Teacher: Should we put the big ones together over here?

The children began to sort large rectangular bricks into one pile. Matthew attempted to put a triangular shaped brick onto the pile.
Jason: Take that away. It's not the same as these.

Example 2
This group of three- and four-year-olds were quite happy on their own, but by listening their teacher was able to learn quite a lot about their use of words and understanding of their meaning. They began to build a roadway using very large hollow blocks.
Jamie: I'll help, because they are heavy, but I'm strong, aren't I?
Simon: And me.
The roadway was soon built with the help of a number of boys.
Jeffrey: Look how long it is.
Paul: We can make it much longer. There are lots more bricks yet.
Alan: Yes. Let's make it longer and longer, till it touches the wall.
When the roadway was finished four of the boys sat on a train to ride along the roadway. Unfortunately as the blocks reached the wall at either side they could not ride on or off at the ends.
Jamie: It's too long. We will have to make it shorter.
Paul: Yes. Let's take some blocks away.
With three blocks removed, it was just the right length for riding on at one end and off at the other.

Example 3

Here the teacher is working with a slightly older group of children and developing sorting, using a sorting box containing cubes, off-cuts of wood, beads, wheels, cotton reels, rods, etc. She asked the children to sort out everything that rolled. Onto one of the trays the children put beads of various sizes, wheels, cotton reels and rods. Pointing to the articles left in the sorting box, the teacher asked, "Why don't these roll?"

Alison (4.9):	Because they are not round.
Teacher:	Are all these round? (Pointing to articles on the tray.)
Children:	Yes.
Teacher:	Are they all the same?
Children:	No.

A further sorting amongst the articles on the tray put them into sets of beads, reels, rods and wheels.

Teacher:	Now, how are they different?
Matthew (4.1):	These are all round [beads] and these are round in the middle [reels].
Teacher:	What about these? (Pointing to rods and wheels.)
Matthew:	Those are round at the end [rods] and those are flat round [wheels].

The final example is perhaps an unexpected mathematical experience as there is no discussion of the tower itself but rather the child has been carried to the top of the high tower in his imagination and asked to look down at the people below. Ian has had this experience in reality and is able to recall it with some explanation.

Example 4

Ian (4.8):	I'm going to build a great big tower to the sky.
Teacher:	If you were right at the top of the tower, what would the people down below you look like?
Ian:	Tidgy.
Teacher:	Why would they look tidgy?
Ian:	Because people do when they are up high.

Perhaps his teacher should have given him a better word than "tidgy", but they both knew what they meant. It is interesting that he replied to her question in reverse!

It is always worth taking a fresh look at the toys and apparatus which are put out daily, to decide just why they are there. For example, placing the blocks in the centre of a large room or out on the porch, instead of in their usual corner, can stimulate quite a different type of play. A whole cupboard may be turned out to find a forgotten toy and then the clearing up, sorting and re-packing becomes an activity in itself.

By deliberately altering the appearance of apparatus which has been put out but not used, a teacher can exploit the sorting and ordering activities that occur when clearing up.

There is sometimes a tendency to set out apparatus at the beginning of a session and then to hurry the clearing up, thus losing valuable experience. It is well worth while to leave plenty of time to help the children to do all the clearing up themselves.

9 Outdoor Activities

Introduction

It is very difficult to generalise on outdoor activities, as the amount of space available differs from school to school. Some have a paved area as small as 10 square metres surrounded by high walls, while others enjoy an orchard, garden, playing field and carefully constructed play spaces. Sometimes the large apparatus can be left outside, always ready for use. In other areas it must be stacked away in sheds or classrooms to avoid the attention of vandals. We usually think of the purely physical and enjoyment value to children of playing in the open air. Indeed, for many children, this may be their first chance to play freely, experiencing hard surfaces, grass, fences, trees, ponds and sand pits.

Just as materials offered to young children in the classroom can be chosen to provide them with experiences leading to the acquisition of mathematical ideas, so the provision and organisation of outdoor activities can encourage children to explore such things as balance, weight, height, depth, direction, speed, spatial order, shape and size with very little participation from an adult.

In ideal situations, indoor and outdoor activities will overlap, as children move freely from one to the other. Bricks, sand, water, paint and dressing-up clothes will, for example, provide different experiences when used out-of-doors.

Many children need to spend much of their time with the group in physical activity out-of-doors, and a teacher supervising them can help to develop their experiences and language, so that she feels her time is being used just as profitably out-of-doors as within the confines of the classroom.

The rapid development of physical co-ordination and agility by children of three and four years old is very obvious. Intellectual development goes hand in hand with this physical progression as children experiment with materials and learn to control them. Their own experience leads them on, for example, to rejecting a full box or bucket that they think is too heavy for them to carry. From being surprised that a ball rolls away on a gentle slope, a child will purposely ride his scooter down the same slope for enjoyment, knowing that he then has to push it up again. The more mature child will be the initiator of imaginative play with boxes, planks and tyres, knowing from past games that certain boxes will fit together and a particular plank will bridge a gap.

This chapter deals with outdoor activities within the school grounds. See chapter 10 *The Environment*, for further outdoor activities, including outings further afield.

Possible developments

Flat, hard surfaces

The old-style playground, tarmac covered, bereft of trees, shrubs, grass and gardens, bounded by a high wall or fence, may be the only outside play space for some groups. Even so, much activity can be encouraged with improvised equipment such as planks, boxes, tyres and barrels.

Toys to ride, and push and pull toys
Scooters, tricycles, bicycles and pedal cars can all be used safely on a flat hard surface and there are many chances for one-to-one correspondence. "Only one on this bike because it's only got one seat", (Simon 4.3).

If a pedal car has two seats, there is room for two and there can also be discussion about front and back.

Whilst riding, children are experiencing various speeds and directions which are influenced by their own body weight and steering ability. Two-, three- and four-wheel toys pose problems of balance. Encourage children to talk about their preference for a particular toy.

With push and pull toys the children experience weight in a very practical way when deciding what and how much they put into a pram or trolley to push.

Example
Darren (3.9) was pushing a friend in a large basket on wheels when his teacher asked if she could have a ride.
Darren: Get in . . . No, I can't push you, you're too heavy!

Different types of barrows and trucks lead children to use them in various ways. It is not easy to give a friend a ride in a wheelbarrow, because of the problems of balance, and it is difficult to carry sand and soil on a trolley with low or slatted sides. Children can find out these differences and we might encourage them to talk about them by posing such questions as:

> How shall we move these planks of wood to the other side of the playground?
> If it rains, do you think that doll will be able to sit up under the hood of the pram?

Many more estimations will be made—rightly or wrongly—by the children as they try to push and pull their prams and trolleys through narrow spaces.

> Do you really think there is room to overtake just there?

Many statements about direction will be made by children while they are pushing and pulling.

> We are all going this way round the tree. You must come behind me.

They also like to up-end push and pull toys for imaginary mending, and wheels can be spun at different speeds.

While playing with the children we can introduce the terms *backwards, forwards, in front of, behind, by the side of* and *next to*. Gradually children will come to understand them in various contexts and so use them in their own play.

Small apparatus

All children love playing with balls and at this age it is sure to be one each, so that one-to-one correspondence comes naturally.

As children mature they may be prepared to share one ball between two, or play with an adult in a small group taking turns at catching or rolling a ball. Bean bags, cloth or woollen balls can all be used and at clearing up time the various balls can be sorted.

Hoops can be used for crawling through, jumping in, out of and over, and comparing sizes. They can also be used for making flat designs on the ground, imaginary steering wheels and stepping stones. At the same time, the children are learning to control them and are finding out some of the properties of a circle.

Skipping ropes are popular and can be used for many activities as well as skipping, jumping over and crawling under.

Two roughly parallel ropes on the ground to jump over. They can be moved further and further apart.

A squiggly rope to jump over. It can wiggle sideways as well as up and down.

Spatial relationships—limited space

Some of the following suggestions may be useful where the space is very limited, while others could be initiated by a teacher with a small group of children who have lost interest in the more usual activities.

Feel all the space around you. Stand close to some other children, now spread out so that you can't touch anybody. Move various parts of you—legs up and down, arms forwards, backwards; look through the arch made by your legs.

Stand against the wall or fence. What can you see? Turn around, now what can you see? A blank wall? Over the top of the wall? Through the fence?

Can we all fit in along this short wall? Now take some big jumps forward. Turn around and jump back to the wall. Let's jump sideways as well as forwards and backwards.

Circles, straight lines and zig-zags can be chalked or painted on to a hard surface for children to walk, run, jump or skip along.

Vocabulary: front – back – forwards – backwards – fast – slow – curved – straight – next to – in front of – behind – by the side of – through – in – out – over – under.

Grassy areas and gardens

Slopes, dips, pathways and steps

A sandbank at the bottom of a steeper incline provides a safe stopping place for bikes and scooters.

Old tyres of various sizes are great fun to roll down slopes, and children can experiment with the different sizes—comparing the speeds and distances.

Pushing the tyres up again takes more energy and children will soon sort out the lightest or compete with one another to push the heaviest.

Many schools are able to make a "jungle" for children, which they love to explore. It may be a shrubbery with a well-trodden path that the children have made themselves or a hard-surfaced path winding between small trees. The children's enjoyment seems to stem from the feeling of being lost, but knowing that they will come out safely at the end. The narrowness of the path means that they must always play "follow the leader", and begin to learn something about position and ordinal number. First, second, third and last will stay in the same order unless there is a junction, when the line may divide and their positions change.

Steps can encourage similar experiences of spatial order as children go up and down and there are also opportunities to make higher and lower comparisons. When trucks and trolleys need to negotiate the steps, children can experience weight, balance and the effect of sharing the weight between several children working together, under the careful supervision of an adult.

Gardens

A garden is useful in helping the children to understand space comparisons and the seasons. Children like to see quick results from their efforts, but a garden, however small, can demonstrate the passing of time as they watch for changes.

A small apple tree, a garden pea or even a strawberry plant pass through various stages during spring and summer and children can look for the first appearance of leaves and flowers and fruit.

> Do the flowers come before the leaves?
> Where will the fruit be?
> When can we eat it?
> How long until it is ripe?
> Are the apples too high for me to reach?

Quick-growing root vegetables such as radishes and carrots which grow out of sight can be compared for size when they are pulled at various times.

> Will some of these carrots grow larger if we leave them till next week?

Children can plant sunflower seeds in pots indoors and then transfer them to the garden in early summer. There they can compare the speed and amount of growth and also compare the height of themselves and adults against the growing plant. Other quick-growing plants are tomatoes and runner beans, but these plants that mature in the autumn are not really suitable for schools that have a long August holiday, as continuity is lost, even if help is available to care for the plants.

Whilst digging in, and planting and weeding the garden, children are bound to find many small creatures, and there are countless opportunities to discuss these. Some topics which may arise are: the length of worms, and their lack of legs; the many legs of a centipede; the slowness of snails and slugs; the woodlouse rolling into a ball; the flight differences of butterflies, bees, ladybirds and flies.

Birds will be attracted to gardens as they hunt for worms, insects, seeds and fruits. Again, differences in sizes, species and habits can be observed.

> Starlings usually come in a noisy crowd, sparrows in twos and threes, while the robin is more often alone.

All these simple garden activities depend upon the real involvement and enjoyment of an adult who loves a garden, and can pass on some of his or her knowledge to children as they work and play together. As they sort weeds from flowers, compare leaves for size and texture and observe symmetries, collect fruits, dig holes for plants and bulbs and arrange stakes and poles, children are absorbing many ideas of spatial order and relationships.

NOTE: When planning a garden, care must be taken to exclude plants which have *poisonous leaves or berries*.

Vocabulary: stop – start – fast – slow – up – down – higher – lower – first – second – third – last.

Shelters

Sunrooms, verandahs and summer-houses give children a feeling of going out and away from the classroom, even in inclement weather. Sometimes this means they have more room for wheel toys, but often it gives them a chance to make their own den to hide away in with a favourite toy.

Wigwams, canvas and tarpaulin shelters need to be erected by adults, but as children help they are experiencing one-to-one correspondence with tapes to loops or hooks to holes, etc. and will soon say:

> There's not enough. You need another one.
> Just two more to do.

The children then have the fun of squeezing themselves and toys inside the shelter and comparisons arise as to how many children can sit, stand or lie down. Again they soon sort this out for themselves.

> You can't come in. You're too fat.
> You can fit in there.
> You can't stand up near the side.

Even more valuable are the shelters that children improvise for themselves. A box with a blanket draped over the top to act as a door makes a home for how many children?

Several boxes and planks with blanket covers pose problems of height, area and weight.

The old-fashioned clothes horse offered to children with a blanket and some clothes pegs lets them explore triangular three-dimensional shapes.

Vocabulary: enough – too many – more than – higher than – lower than – inside – outside – in – out – over – under.

Large apparatus

Opinions vary widely as to safety of various pieces of large apparatus. Most of the equipment must be locked away in storerooms and sheds at night and put out again every morning. When the children help, they sometimes suggest a different way of arranging things and even a small alteration can suddenly make a forgotten toy more popular. Some of the mathematical ideas which can be experienced with the most general apparatus are suggested here.

Climbing frames

These are often fixed, but a movable ladder can be hooked on different sides to encourage children to look in different directions.

The square, window-type frame gives practice with moving in and out as well as up, down and over the top of, and there is experience of being enclosed within a three-dimensional shape.

When I climbed up here yesterday, I could see the church. Today I can see the shops.
What shall I see if I climb round here?

Scrambling nets need more awareness and control of body weight than fixed frames.

Slides

Slides can also be pointed in various directions and if there are several, with different gradients, more comparisons of body control can be made. Body position can also be varied; sitting or lying face in or face up is safer than head first.

Swings

There are a great many different swings, but a child must be aware of the skill necessary to make a swing work, that is, transference of his own body weight, as he goes forwards, backwards, up, down and sideways. Some swings have seats of various heights, others have double handgrips or a rubber tyre. There are single ropes to curl around and seats on single ropes.

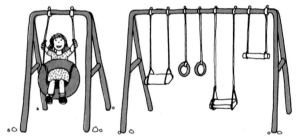

They all provide different experiences that children can be encouraged to talk about.

Seesaws

Seesaws and swingboats both lead to estimation of weight as children look for a comfortable partner. A too-heavy

friend will put Jane up in the air all the time until they learn to balance their weight by sitting in different positions.

Tunnels

Barrels, and tunnels made from large pipes, can either be flat on the ground or raised on frames so that steps or sloping planks are needed to get into them.

Children learn to change their own shapes as they go from one to another and also gain further experience of spatial order, as overtaking is impossible and "first in, first out" becomes the rule. More timid children who are just watching can be encouraged to remember who went into the tunnel first and watch for them coming out again.

Improvised

Cardboard cartons, discarded beer and milk crates, bread baskets, planks, bricks and other builder's waste, old tyres and steering wheels can all be made safe for children to experiment with as they build and imagine themselves as pilots, racing drivers, farmers and naval captains. All the time they are experimenting with weight, size and shape in three dimensions.

Boxes

Boxes, hidey-holes and box steps can be fitted together or used separately and children usually help to arrange these themselves, again giving many opportunities to experience "inside", "outside", "on top of", "next to", "in front of" and "behind".

Boats and vehicles

Some nurseries have old boats and vehicles which have been made safe for children to play in. Experience of "inside", "outside", "up", "down", "under" and "over" will arise here, as well as the number of children who can get in.

Trees

Tree stumps to jump from, logs to climb over and smaller logs to arrange in patterns and roll about, give experiences of height, weight, and shape.

Vocabulary: in – out – up – down – through – on top of – next to – in front of – behind – heavy – light – first – last – over – under – inside – outside.

Sand pits

Shape

The shape of a sand pit is usually decided by the space and materials available, but if planning a new one, here are some ideas that may help to make it even more exciting. Strong, but not "too heavy to move", covers must be provided unless the area is absolutely cat, dog and vandal proof. Hexagonal, curved or irregularly shaped pits are more interesting than square ones. It may be possible to prepare the pit with a sloping bottom so that deeper holes can be dug at one end, leading to comparisons being made. A paved or cement area next to the pit makes a good surface for sand castles and another paved area, at a little distance from the pit, to use as a dumping place for sand-filled trucks, encourages imaginative play.

Equipment

Experiences leading to mathematical ideas can be encouraged by providing a range of equipment in various sizes. Buckets in different sizes, as well as colours, encourage conversation between the children and between the children and adults.

> "Mine will be the largest sand castle."
> "Oh dear, it's too heavy for me to lift."

Spades of various sizes encourage children to see who can fill buckets of the same size first, or dig the deepest holes.

Children often match the colours of their equipment, but sometimes the smallest spade is the same colour as the largest bucket and further conversation can be encouraged as they discover it is not always easier to fill a small bucket with a large spade, than to fill a large bucket with a small spade.

Rakes, pounders, sticks, boxes and sieves will all produce interesting shapes and tracks in the sand, leading to guessing games such as, "Guess what I did this with".

Marks made by feet can be compared.

> This must be a giant's foot. Look at it next to my foot!

Imaginative play

While this should never be interrupted by a mathematically obsessed adult, provision of suitable equipment and the space to use it will lead children to make many useful discoveries.

> If we fill the wheelbarrow with sand in the pit, it's too heavy to lift out.

This is the tallest castle I've ever built. Now I'll stand on the top. Now I'll make a tunnel underneath it. That's the doorway. My leg can go right inside.

Children will learn about weight, volume, length, shape and size, and gain some idea of the invariance of mass as they move sand from one container to another.

Vocabulary: full – empty – heavy – light – deep – shallow – match – on top of – underneath.

Ponds and paddling pools

Some schools have permanent pools outside, but as with the sand pit, they need to be kept clean and free from intruders. Many of the mathematical ideas connected with them are described in chapter 5 *Water*.

The weather

The amount of time spent out of doors is so dependent upon the weather that children are bound to be aware of changes and some effects of sun, wind, rain and snow.

Sun
What is a shadow? Children can look for shadows of trees, walls, houses, swings, climbing frames, etc., comparing the shape of the original with its shadow. Shadows of themselves, adults and smaller children can be compared. Games of chasing shadows, jumping on someone else's shadow, making tall and short shadows, can all be initiated by an adult with a small group of interested children.

When does the sun make us feel hot? Some comparisons of the seasons can be included here and sunny or shady parts of the garden sorted out for various times of the day.

Wind
How strong is the wind today?
Are the leaves being blown from the trees?
Is the washing moving on the clothes line?
Which way is the wind blowing?
Is it blowing us backwards or forwards?
Let's make some paper windmills. Which way do they go round more quickly?
Let's fly a kite or blow some bubbles up into the sky.

Rain
Rainwater can be collected in different-sized containers, raindrops observed going down window panes, etc. For further suggestions, see chapter 5 *Water*.

Snow
Nearly all children want to go out in the snow and, if they are suitably dressed, they can have many mathematically rewarding experiences as well as lots of fun. They can compare the weight of some loose snow on one hand with a compressed snowball on the other. They can use snow to make a big ball or snowman.

They can make tracks and footmarks in the snow, and on finding footmarks can guess which way the person who made them was going.

Buckets can be filled with snow—loosely or hard packed—and the amount of water found when the snow has melted can be discussed and compared.

If there is enough snow to make a really big snowman, he may be as tall as Mr A. on the first day, but as he melts, he will shrink to be as tall as Miss B. and then as small as the smallest child, until he finally disappears.

Vocabulary: inside – outside – behind – forwards – backwards – full – empty.

The teacher's role

With outdoor activities, even more than indoors, the good teacher becomes the provider of materials and the involved observer. Many children are quite happy to run, push, pull, ride and climb, but when an adult is standing by, ready to help, she is sure to be drawn in by the children as in the following example.

Example 1
In the outside sand pit, the teacher sat down to dig, using a small spade. Timothy (4.2) handed the teacher a large spade and said, "Use this one; it digs deeper."

Younger children, or those that have had little experience of playing freely, need a little more encouragement and the next example illustrates how a teacher was able to lead a small group without directing them too much.

Example 2
Zahid (3.11) was playing in the sand pit in the playground, one of a group of four children, with a teacher, engaged in digging a trench around a log.
Zahid: (Upon completing the job) All round now.
Teacher: Yes, it goes all the way round the log now. We can make this piece higher if you want to. (Indicating island in the middle)
Zahid: Yes, higher.
Finally, the teacher took a bucket and made a sand castle on top. Zahid took another, and made a second castle.
Zahid: Two now!

In the next example the boys, with the pedal car, had already made their decision on size and did not really need the teacher to question them about it, but they were obviously quite used to talking with her.

Example 3
Christopher (4.7) was riding in the pedal car with Mark (4.7) pushing. When they got near the large boxes, Christopher stood up inside the car and lifted it round to turn it. The teacher asked why they lifted it round.

Christopher: We can't get round there. (Pointing to the boxes)
Teacher: Why not?
Christopher: There isn't enough room. There's a big box there.
Mark: Can't get round there. There isn't enough room.

Perhaps she could have continued the conversation by offering to move the boxes or asking them how much more room they needed, and how it could be found.

The next teacher provided some different materials and left the children to experiment. She writes about some of the things that happened.

Example 4

One day I put some large heavy cardboard tubes in the wheelbarrows and awaited the reaction from the children first coming out to play. At first the boys went straight for the cars as usual and the girls didn't notice. One boy (4.8) said "What's those things?"

Paul (3.8) pushed the wheelbarrow with the tubes inside and on reaching the small slide stopped and tried rolling them down it. He then tried putting them on the roll-about tyre. Then he put them on his arms, grew tired and left them.

Rebecca (3.10) rolled them along the ground.

Sarah (4.9) and Donna (3.11) put them in and out of the wheelbarrow.

Julian (4.5) and David (4.2) stood them up and played a game with them as rockets going up to the sky. They then tried sitting on them. They put them on their arms, but Julian noticed his were of different lengths, one covering his hand, the other leaving his hand extended beyond the edge. He did not like this and changed them for two of the same length. Later they had them set in a row near the climbing frame. They were of three different heights so in conversation with Julian I asked if they were all the same height or if some were taller than the others. Julian, although knowing through putting them on his arms that they were of different lengths, said they were "the same". Sarah was watching and listening so I asked her if she thought they were all the same. She said, "No, that one is the biggest", picking out the tallest one. I asked which were the next tallest and she picked out the only two of the

next size. I asked which were the smallest, and she picked out the three shortest ones quickly.

The next day Julian found the tubes again and started to put his arms in them to play "Daleks". Donna joined him and he found her the shortest ones, saying, "You have the short ones. You are small."

Later Julian and David took them and stood them along the ground near the climbing frame. Julian then found by laying three equal sized tubes end to end, they would exactly fit along a double bar between two uprights and would not roll off because the bars were near and parallel to each other. He then tried propping the others up on the climbing frame but they kept falling off. He could not suggest why this should happen. When one rolled along the ground he picked it up and stood it on its end to stop it rolling.

The teacher had chosen her time to join them with the purpose of extending their mathematical thinking and the second day's activity shows that David had absorbed some of the ideas about size.

Example 5

Teacher:	Shall we make a monster's shadow, children.
Caroline (4.5):	How can we, we haven't got a monster?
Teacher:	Make a line. Now stand exactly behind the person in front of you. Look, you've made a long shadow. Now hold your arms out. Look at the shadow. What can you see?
Carolyn (4.6):	Look, it's a big crocodile.
Maxine (4.6):	It looks like a real monster.
Teacher:	Wave your arms about and see what happens.
Katherine (4.2):	Look—it's moving. It's a crawly thing.

Again, the following mathematical thoughts would not have been explored and put into words without the right question from Gillian's teacher.

Example 6
Gillian (4.6) was one of three children playing in the large paddling pool in the garden, when she commented (whilst gently stirring the water with her feet), "Oh, the water's heavier than my feet."
Teacher: How can you tell?
Gillian: Well, it's lifting my feet up.

On the other hand, Peter initiates the next conversation by asking the question. His teacher's explanation would help to consolidate his previous experiences.

Example 7
Peter (4.9) was on the tyre with wheels.
Peter: Why did you go backwards when I was coming to you?
Teacher: You were coming towards me and I thought you were going to run me over, Peter. If I'd moved forwards, we would have bumped.
Peter: I'll go backwards now.

Example 8
Teacher: What is that shape on the playground?
Leanne (4.5):   My shadow.
Teacher: How can you tell that it is your shadow?
Leanne: It's joined on to me, it starts at my feet.
Teacher: Is your shadow the same shape as you?
Leanne: Yes. Look it's got two legs and it's got two plaits the same as me.
Teacher: What will happen to your shadow if you move?
Leanne: (Swinging body from side to side) It moves with me, look.

Teacher: Let's see what happens if you jump.
Leanne: Look it's jumping with me.
Teacher: Do you think your shadow is the same size as you, Leanne?
Leanne: It looks the same, I think it is.
Teacher: Shall we see if it is?
The teacher then took a length of string, cut it to the height of the child and laid it on the ground on top of the shadow of Leanne.
Leanne: Oh, my shadow's bigger than me.

This incident has led to work being carried on, comparing shadow sizes. Lunchtime, milktime and hometime sizes are being measured and chalk outlines made.

Example 9
The teacher demonstrated shadow animals using hands, and this led to further experiment with shadows.
Teacher: Let's play some tricks with our shadows. Maxine, look at your shadow. Now, has this bucket got a shadow?
Maxine (4.6):   Yes, I can see it by mine.
Teacher: Put your hand down here. (Teacher guided hand in front of bucket handle) Now look at the shadows. What does it look as if you are going to do?
Maxine: It looks like I'm going to pick it up, but I'm not. My hand's not really at the back. It's at the front.

Observing the children's play out of doors, teachers will be able to draw in and encourage some children by offering them small problems to solve, such as the best way to move some bricks from one side of the garden to another. As they become more independent, she can, by the provision of suitable equipment and conversation, lead them on to explore many mathematical ideas while their physical skills are developing.

10 The Environment

Introduction

There are a number of ways in which adults can help to widen children's experience by taking them out into the community and letting them see other people going about their daily work. In small parties, conversation flows naturally as they explore new places, and some of this is sure to be about distance, size, speed, shape and number. Many mathematical ideas may be absorbed as children observe, question, look for differences and make comparisons. On returning, or even some time later, they may recall some of these as they talk about their experiences and try to recreate them in paint, clay or junk materials.

Other chapters in this book point out many of the mathematical ideas that can be developed from the everyday activities and the first part of this chapter explores the immediate vicinity.

But very soon, children are ready to find out about the world outside. Gradually, as short outings come to be taken for granted, they can be planned with a particular object in mind. Of course, this will not always be mathematical.

Expeditions can be divided into two main categories. First, there are those that can be last-minute decisions. A gale may have blown down some trees and children can watch workmen chopping, sawing and burning. A visit to the shops, although planned, may perhaps be postponed if bad weather or staff difficulties arise, and put on again at short notice. Such expeditions, usually undertaken with a few

children and one or two adults, can be fitted into part of a morning or afternoon. Here are some suggestions of areas to visit: 1 Shopping areas; 2 Residential areas; 3 Busy streets; 4 Open spaces, parks and playing fields.

Other expeditions are longer and require more planning, as transport and extra adult helpers may need to be organised and arrangements made with the staff of the chosen place. Some successful expeditions with small groups of children have been concerned with: 5 A farm; 6 A zoo; 7 A railway station; 8 Canals, rivers and sea-shore; 9 People working.

As well as meeting the world outside, children can be encouraged to take an interest in the various people who come into the school, for example the doctor, nurse, dentist, milkman, postman, builder and dinner-man. Parents, grandparents and other relatives are sometimes willing to bring examples of their work and talk to the children.

Possible developments

Shopping area

Small shops

Visits to smaller shops for shopping, or just to look, lead to simple ideas of *sorting*, such as, "I like this, but I don't like that".

The following suggestions contain questions which may be asked by the children, or similar ones could be put by the adults to stimulate further interest in seeing *differences* which in turn leads on to *sorting* and the making of *sets*.

Many housing estates and small villages have one general shop which may also serve as the post office. Young children may already be very familiar with this shop and quite used to spending their pennies on sweets and ice-cream. But a visit with an adult who has time to stop and look in the window could be a treat. How many different kinds of things can be seen? Sweets? Apples? Toys? Writing paper? Birthday cards? Tins? Boxes?

A small parade of specialist shops will provide more examples. Butter and sugar will come from the grocer, but where shall we buy cabbages and onions? Which is the right shop for buying toothpaste?

Let's look at the shoe shop. Are there shoes for daddy? Are they different from my shoes? Are they different from your shoes?

This is the wool shop. The colours are all in separate little boxes on the wall. Why aren't they all mixed up?

What is the next shop called? Not a meat shop, but a butcher's shop. Let's think of some things that he doesn't sell. Newspapers? Apples? Hair ribbons?

After an expedition of this type, children may begin to sort through various boxes and empty packets in the junk materials container. As they recognise Corn Flake boxes, toothpaste and talcum powder boxes, etc. the adult can join their play and ask if they remember which shop they would come from.

Much incidental mathematical conversation can arise on visits to the shops, as can be seen in the following example, where the children are comparing routes and ideas of left and right are introduced.

Example

Joanne (4.2): We come to school this way, you know.
Sarah (4.7): I've been this way before, but when I go shopping I go this way. (Points to left)

The supermarket

This is an entirely different outing from that just described, as instead of asking a shopkeeper for a certain item, the shopper must find it for himself, sorting out size, variety and number.

If a number of items is needed, and a quiet time chosen, perhaps the children could each carry their own basket. The teacher in the example below gave each child in the group a picture of the item they were to find by matching.

Example

Shaleni (4.4):	I've found the flour.
Teacher:	Is it the same as your picture?
Shaleni:	(Pointing) That isn't, but this is.

The open market

This can be a very exciting place for a few children with an adult, before the crowds arrive.

Shape and size   The stalls need to be erected—look at the way they open up, and at the struts, spars, nuts, bolts and trestles. Shapes, sizes, angles and covers can all be looked at and compared.

Comparisons   As the articles to be sold are put out, the children can look at the various containers.

That sack of potatoes must be very heavy. The man carried it on his back.

Look at the enormous bundle that lady has put on the table. What shall we see when she undoes the knots? What a lot of pieces of different material.

That man sells wheels. That one would be the right size for my dad's bike and that one would do for our doll's pram.

Sorting   The man has put all the hammers at this end and the screwdrivers next to them. He has some nails to sell and we need them for our woodwork. Shall we buy long or short nails? Let's ask for a mixed packet so that we can sort them out when we get back to school.

There are all sorts of different things on this stall. I can see some bottles. They are not like our milk bottles or our squash bottles. Are they old ones? My granny keeps her salt in a jar like that. These are funny old saucepans; let's see if we can find the right lids to fit on them.

We have discussed just a few of the ideas that may arise as children explore the market. Children who are used to asking questions will need very little prompting, while the younger or less mature may be happy to watch until prompted by an adult who, for example, wonders why the man keeps all the oranges in a box instead of putting them out on the table?

Vocabulary: beginning – end – the same as – different – holds more than – is heavier than – enough – too many – as much as – flat – full – empty – some – all – longer – shorter.

Residential areas

Short walks with one or two children will offer more ideas. The flats are taller than the houses, but are the houses taller than the bungalows?

Sorting   All the doors of the flats are the same shape. Are they the same colour too? Are the doors of the houses the same shape? How many different colours can we see? What is different about bungalows?

Look at the shapes around us. Some round things that may be spotted include: petrol caps, road signs, lights on cars, manhole covers, clocks, balls, pebbles, letter-boxes, waste bins and wheels on cars, prams and bicycles.

Children who come to school by car or bus rarely have time to look at the gardens of houses close to a school in a residential area. A short walk could start with a simple objective, for example, to look for gardens that have daffodils. Some gardens will only have one or two daffodils, others will have a great many. The seasons, time and speed of growth are all sure to be mentioned in conversation with children.

During a walk, some of the regular tradesmen may be seen making their deliveries. Watch the *milkman* delivering full bottles and removing empty ones. Look at his float and try to decide whether he is near the beginning or end of his round. Has he more empty bottles or full bottles?

The *coalman* may be delivering sacks of coal. Count the empty bags as he puts them in a pile.

Perhaps a *baker* will be seen delivering to the shop. Does he take more bread to a shop than to a house?

Example
Stephen (4.4): He [the baker] just gets in and goes and then he stops and gets out.
Gary (4.2): Well, it isn't far to the next house.

The *postman* may be delivering letters. Does he go to all the houses? Perhaps it will be the right time for the postman to empty the letter-box. Look at all the letters—all different shapes and sizes.

The *dustman* goes to every house and flat. Is there always one bin or sack from each house, or more? If the bins are left along the street outside the houses there may be some discussion on how "all that rubbish can get into the van". The crushing mechanism may lead the children to experiment back at school—finding how much newspaper may be squashed into a sack, or how many flattened cardboard cartons can fit into a box.

Estimation of size Somebody is moving house. Will all their furniture go into that van? Let's see how the men fit it all in. Some pieces are too heavy for one man to carry. It needs two men to carry the wardrobe.

Vocabulary: lower than – higher than – more than – up – down – less than – outside – inside – how many? – before – after – full – empty – too much – how much? – all – some.

Busy streets

Roadworks
All sorts of construction work is interesting for children to watch and they can make many discoveries from a safe distance.

Comparisons and shape The vehicles are wide, long, high, have double wheels, big wheels, or different sizes of wheels. Pipes are cylindrical. Some holes are deeper/wider than others. Some holes have rims that are square, some rectangular, some circular. Look at road signs.

Movements There are machines that dig down, lift up, turn over, press flat and make trenches. As they negotiate the works, machines go backwards, forwards, over, near, far away and through.

Road junctions
Using pedestrian subways and footbridges may lead to conversation about under and over. There are differences in speeds to watch for as traffic slows down and stops at traffic lights or pedestrian crossings.

Bus stops
Position The people in the bus queue are in front of or behind each other. Will they all get on the bus? Will some wait for a different bus? Who is first in the queue now? Who is second, third, last? A short ride on a bus, paying for tickets and finding seats, will make the expedition even more exciting and mathematically valuable.

Counting
Some children like to count the vehicles, if a safe spot can be found to watch from. Other children may like to drop a counter or small brick into a box with an appropriate picture (car, lorry, bus, etc.) as they spot a particular vehicle. This is a matching or one-to-one correspondence

exercise that may culminate in a purely visual comparison of the final amounts. For example, "the car box is full, but the bus box is nearly empty".

Symmetry and perspective   Junk constructions and paintings give children a chance to show their appreciation of symmetry and balance as they place wheels in position. When painting, if they reach the stage of saying "You can't see the wheels on the other side" they are also showing their ideas on perspective. Piaget's work (Jean Piaget and Barbel Inhelder, *The Child's Conception of Space*, Chapters I, II, VI, X, Routledge & Kegan Paul, 1956) indicates that children do not really understand perspective until they are seven-, eight- or nine-years-old. *Checking Up II* (Nuffield Mathematics Project, *Checking Up II*, Summary Check-up No. 2, W. & R. Chambers, 1972) also contains suggestions for a game with older children to see how they use the terms "in front of", "behind", etc.

Vocabulary: backwards – forwards – over – near – through – wide – long – high – down – up – circle – triangle – under – first – second – third – last – in front of – behind.

Open spaces, parks and playing fields

Parks
Comparisons   Trees can be tall, thick, straight or curved, and can have branches near the ground or a long way up. Parts of the roots can be above ground providing holes "big enough for a rabbit" (Victoria, 4.11), or which have "only enough room for a mouse" (Christopher, 4.7).

Trying to climb up a gnarled oak tree, some children thought they had gone really high when their feet were level with other children's shoulders.

Discuss the relative sizes of different pitches, e.g. football pitch or tennis court.

Where trees have been sawn down, or there are logs, the annular rings will interest children. They can trace them with their fingers and also compare the smooth feel with the outside bark.

Sorting   Leaves of all varieties can be collected and sorted for size, shape, colour, texture and quantity.

Example

Nigel (4.9):	Some leaves are big, some small, some middle sized.
Michelle (4.10):	They are different shapes. Some are round and curly.
Andrew (4.9):	Some have got straight sides, some are spikey, some have stalks on.
Nigel:	All of them have got stalks on. Leaves grow off branches.

Small streams and ditches
Ideas of depth and width   Small streams and ditches need to be crossed or skirted. A small party of four-year-olds, wearing rubber boots, didn't wait to answer their teacher's questions of "How are we going to get to the other side? Shall we go over or round?" They started off—through!

Christopher did not appear to estimate the depth of the water or steepness of the further bank, but went ahead confidently. Victoria watched him and must have seen that the water did not reach very far up his rubber boots, but she still needed reassurance that it "was not very deep". At a gateway, the water from the ditch apparently disappeared, until further investigation showed that it went into a pipe under the footpath, and out of the pipe to the next ditch.

Natural areas
Collections and sorting   Children love to collect something to take back to school, e.g. pebbles, feathers, small twigs.

Back at school these can be sorted in various ways, e.g. size, weight, texture, from plant/animal, from ground level, above or below.

It is never too early to introduce the idea of conservation and children should be discouraged from collecting living plants and taking twigs from trees.

Hills

Children enjoy climbing up and running down. The steepness of one hill might be compared with that of another, and from the top of a hill children may look down and comment upon the seeming smallness of cars on a motorway or animals in a field.

Vocabulary: thick – thin – above – below – deep – shallow – into – out of – last – corner – edge (perimeter) – first – second – third – higher – lower – longer – shorter.

The farm

Rubber boots, raincoats and even a packed lunch may lead to conversations about the weather. There may also be some appreciation of the length of time needed to get to and from the farm.

There will be differences to be seen between animals that roam freely most of the time, e.g. sheep, cows, horses and chickens, and those that are in pens, e.g. pigs, calves, turkeys. There will be differences in textures to feel, if the children are able to touch the animals. They may be able to collect pieces of sheep's wool and hair from horses' tails from hedges and fences. Many different feathers and other bric-à-brac can be collected and sorted. On their return to school, children will also have a new interest in sorting the toy animals in their farmyard.

Outings to a farm provide many opportunities for comparisons. Children may begin to estimate the size of the animals and describe them as "taller than me" or "small enough to carry".

One group of children taken to a dairy farm, actually "measured" a cow by standing beside it with outstretched arms: "It took John and me to go from its nose to its tail!" On returning to the school, Jane (4.10) painted this picture and said "We measured the cows like this."

Follow-up

Friezes and collages made after a farm visit will lead to counting, sorting and comparing. The children might count the number of legs on a horse, a cow and a chicken, or the number of separate fields or pens to be made. Selection of coloured materials or suitable "junk" shapes for collage will involve sorting.

Vocabulary: taller than – longer than – fatter than – smaller than – inside – outside – heavier than – different.

The zoo

This is another expedition that will need planning and should involve a large ratio of adults to children. During the preparation time there may be talk about money for fares, admission fees and, perhaps, drinks.

If there are sufficient adults, it is probably better for the children to split up into very small groups of two or three with an adult, so that each party can go at its own speed, seeing separate parts of the zoo and so providing many experiences to recall on their return to school.

Comparisons   Do all animals and birds have tails? Which animals have the longest, shortest, thickest, thinnest or curliest tails? Do some animals have tails that are longer than their bodies?

Which animals have ponds or water in their enclosures because they like to be in or under the water?

Look at the fences and wire netting. Are there different heights, patterns and thicknesses?

Look for different sizes and shapes of animals' houses. How do the sizes of doorways compare? Do some animals have a larger enclosure? Is there just one animal/bird in each enclosure or are there two or many?

Shape   Watch the way that animals and birds stand and move. Notice that our own knees always bend forwards.

Look for the knees of a crocodile, ostrich, lion, etc.

There are so many exciting things to see and talk about at the zoo that mathematical ideas are bound to be experienced by just talking about animals, birds, and reptiles that are "bigger than", "smaller than", "like", "stronger than", "run faster than", "climb higher than" each other. Animal families may be seen. Comments from some nursery children on seeing a one-week-old giraffe included:

He's not as big as his mum.
He's not as tall as his mummy's leg.
Hasn't he got tiny feet?

For the really curious child (or adult) *The Guinness Book of Animal Facts and Feats* (ed. G. L. Wood, *The Guinness Book of Animal Facts and Feats*, Guinness, 1972) gives the answer to many questions. Some zoos have their own Educational Adviser who is always ready to help plan a really profitable and enjoyable day at the zoo.

Follow-up work usually includes paintings, friezes, collages and model-making. The ideas for sorting are endless, e.g. tails/no tails; wings/no wings; bigger than me/smaller than me; fur/skin, etc.

Vocabulary: two – three – four – six – eight – ten – many – high up – low down – larger than – smaller than – inside – outside – indoors – outdoors.

The railway station

A trip to the station and perhaps a ride in a train will be new experiences for many young children and here are some of the mathematical ideas that one group of children talked about during their outing.

At the first station

There are four lines. They look straight. They go a long way. The platform is higher than the lines. The bridge goes over the line.

Those two ladies were late. They nearly missed the train.

How will they get the pram on to the train? There are big doors in the guard's van. One has to be wide open to get the pram through.

Buying tickets at the machine gives experience of one-to-one correspondence—one ticket for each person.

On the train
It goes slowly first, then faster and faster.

The houses and flats look small. They are tall now we are close to them.
That train's on another track because it's going the other way.

The sun is following us.

At the destination
This is a smaller station.

There are two tracks. We came this way, we go home that way.

The platform is high up so the steps go down to the road. We can look down on fields, trees, a bridge and buildings.

The hills are a long way away, but we can see them, and they do not look very high.

Coming home
The signal goes up and the train goes through. The train stops when the signal is down.

The goods train has more wagons than we can count.

Example
The seats on the train were facing backwards.
Stuart (4.6): "We're looking back where we've come from."

Example
The train had passed under a railway bridge on leaving the station.
Dean (4.4): I go to my home under a bridge, and it's an arch.
Teacher: What's an arch?

Dean: It's like this. (Moves his hand in a semi-circle)
Mark (4.0): The bridge is very high. It has to be for the buses.

Canals, rivers and seashore

For children who live near a canal or a river, a small party on an organised outing will encounter many different experiences, and the ideas which follow have been taken from children's conversation with their teachers on such an expedition.

We saw some high boats and little boats.
We have seen two streams going very fast and a very fast waterfall.
That would be deep enough for a whale to swim in.
The boat's going slowly under the bridge.
The canal isn't going as fast as the stream.
The boat has to go backwards for the gate to open.
This is a pull-up bridge, then boats can go underneath.
This is a narrow boat. This is a very long boat.
Some boats are in a long line.

Vocabulary: straight – higher than – over – under – slowly – fast – backwards – forwards – as far as – deep enough – narrow – wide.

People working

Children enjoy short expeditions to see people at work, and some of the incidental mathematics they experience is suggested here. Most of it will concern the making of comparisons but there may also be opportunities for recognising numbers, counting, and making estimations of height, length, depth, area, volume and weight.

A garage

The cars are in order, waiting to go through the car wash. You must be quick after you've put the money in. If you are not quick enough you get very wet.

The car is on the ramp. It goes up slowly. It is higher up than the man. Now he can see underneath, he won't have to bend down.

The petrol pump has a clock. Watch and count as the hand goes round.

A breaker's yard

Look at all those tyres. See all the different sizes.

Look at the squashed up cars. They don't take up as much room.

That car is high up in the air on a crane.

A building site

Point out that a very large clear space is needed to build houses. Notice that the shapes of the foundations are pegged out. Watch the cement mixer working. The cement comes down the chute, into the bucket, onto the pile, into wheelbarrows or into trenches. Watch the workmen smoothing the cement flat. How many spadesful of cement are needed to fill a wheelbarrow?

Lorries can be sorted by size, colour, use, noisiness, etc.

Bricks are stacked up in a pile. They are built up in a pattern. One brick is halfway over the one underneath.

The post office

We need money to buy a stamp. Some stamps cost more than others. Shall we get any change?

We can't post a parcel into the letter-box.

The parcel must be weighed. It will cost more money than a letter. It is heavy.

There are numbers on the telephone dials. This is my number.

A caravan centre

What a small caravan. It's too small to have stairs. Where are the beds? This one fits me. We need two more beds.

Example

Alison (3.4):   There is a mammy daddy bed.
Christina (4.2):   And there is an up and a down, like I sleep in.

The library

Some of these books are like the ones we have at school. There are chairs to sit on that are just the right size. The books that are higher up are for older boys and girls. The little cards are for all the people who borrow the books. We can count the fire extinguishers. Why do they need so many?

Other outings could include a bakery, a fire station, a bus station, a forge, a pet shop, the baby clinic, a laundrette or a café. The children will acquire many mathematical ideas including sorting, matching, ordering and making comparisons, as they explore their environment with adults who are ready to talk with them.

Example

Some children were looking at photographs taken during their expedition.

Marina (5.0):   Look how small we look next to the doors.
James (5.0):   We only look small like that because you stood a long way away to take the photograph.

Vocabulary: order – one behind another – underneath – count – size – halfway – square – down – under – over – more – older – taller – higher – straight – lower – on top of.

The teacher's role

In exploring the environment, the enthusiasm and fore-thought of the teacher is all-important. Everything new is exciting to young children, but a little extra planning can make it mathematically stimulating as well. A child can become aware of himself and his body in relation to a building whether he is inside, outside, at the top or at ground level. He begins to get an idea of perspective as he views the landscape from various vantage points and experiences various speeds as he travels by car, bus, boat or train. The little girl in Example 1 was having her first ride on a train and made some interesting discoveries. The adult tried to develop her thoughts.

Example 1

Andrea (4.7):   Cor, I've never been on a train before.
Adult: Not when you went to Hungary?
Andrea: No—a boat then, and a car. This is great. Oh look, are those flats taller than us in the train?
Adult: What do you think?
Andrea: Yes, they are tall now they are close to us.
Adult: What about those houses?
Andrea: Those look small.
Adult: Why?
Andrea: Because they are a long way away.

After seeing real machines, some children try to reproduce them from junk materials and in the next story Bernadette is led to think just a little more carefully about wheels.

Example 2

Bernadette (4.3) was making a car on the woodwork bench. She selected four similar-sized plastic carton tops for wheels.

Bernadette: Cars have all the same size wheels.
Teacher: Do all things with wheels have the same-sized wheels?
Bernadette: Yes.
Teacher: Even tractors?
Bernadette: Tractors have big wheels because they cut the grass. The grass is long.

It is not always necessary or indeed desirable to talk to children as they are making discoveries. By taking a group of children to an interesting place, the teacher in Example 3 was able to hear their conversation as they made "rubbings", using thick crayons and kitchen paper.

Example 3
Shaleni (4.4): This path is rough.
Susan (4.2): It's all lumpy.
Shaleni: I'll hold the paper.
Susan: Look at the wriggly line.
Simon (3.9): There's a pattern on the stairs. It makes a rough feel.
Kate (3.3): This has got bumps on it. Look, the crayon bumps up and down.

It did not matter if the paper was torn or discarded, the value was in the doing and experience of various textures. In the next example, the conversation, during a walk shows how an idea can gradually develop and one needn't just talk about squares and rectangles!

Example 4
The teacher pointed to the fire hydrant sign.
Teacher: Do you know what that is?
Gary (4.2): It's a square.
Teacher: Yes, it's a special square to tell the firemen that there is a tap under the pavement ... We'll look out for other hydrant signs.
Gary: This is a rectangle. (Pointing to the hydrant manhole)

After the next hydrant sign was pointed out the children began to see the signs quickly even before getting right up to them.

Stephen (4.4): It isn't very far [to the next hydrant].

Teacher: If there weren't many hydrants the fire engine would have to have a very long hose to stretch from the tap in the ground to the fire if it wasn't near.
Gary: The hydrants are on corners [of the road].
Teacher: That is so that the hose can stretch up any of the roads.
John (4.3): Up there and up there and up there and up there. (Pointing up each road)
Gary: That is four ways.

When returning to the school Gary said, "We'll not find any more [hydrants] because we are back to our own."

During their time in school, children will continue to find new interests in their immediate environment and will enjoy occasional longer journeys. They will absorb a certain amount of road sense by being taken for walks along busy as well as quiet thoroughfares by reliable adults who have the time, patience and forethought to make simple journeys eventful. Just as every child is different, so is every class or group of children. The town child needs to know about his own neighbourhood, as well as being taken into the country and the reverse is just as true for the child from a small village.

Nevertheless, the teacher must always ask herself one question—What experiences will the children gain from this expedition that they could not get from anywhere else? Obviously the answer will not always be mathematical, but practical experiences of distance, size, speed, temperature, height and weight will almost certainly arise.

11 The Passage of Time

Introduction

One of the most difficult concepts for a young child to grasp is that of the *passage of time*. "Time" cannot be seen, nor can it be measured directly. In fact, one can only measure a period of time by first allowing it to pass.

Children live in the present and while they are busy with an activity, they take each moment as it comes. They are not concerned that other children and adults are able to engage in their own activities at the same time. Then, suddenly, they see that a change has occurred—a change which may be heralded by the introduction of a new activity, a change in the weather, the commencement of hunger pains or, eventually, by the movement of clock hands. The introduction of a regular, though not rigid, routine enables the children to begin to understand that events do progress in an ordered, inter-related way.

We cannot always tell if children fail to remember the sequence of events or just lack the vocabulary to express themselves. But the right question, as in the following example, leads a child on to recall events and show that he can remember and predict what he expects to happen.

Example
David (3.9): When I go home from school, I go to bed.
Teacher: You don't go straight to bed, though, do you?
David: No, I have my tea and watch the telly first.

It is from early experiences which introduce ideas such as "before", "after", "how long", "how soon" that children gradually acquire the notion of the passage of time and its measurement. Time is also bound up with the first ideas of speed and rates of growth. Most children acquire a vocabulary of time words from their environment, but it is usually a long time before they understand their meaning. The ideas introduced in the next section may help in the gaining of this understanding.

Dinner time

143

Possible developments

In the classroom, many situations arise through which children may be led to an appreciation of the nature of time and its passage.

The daily routine

All schools have a daily routine in which the children find a great deal of security. This routine can be a help in displaying the link between events and the passing of time.

Before school

It would be wrong to assume that every child comes to the classroom at nine o'clock after a leisurely walk, following an unhurried breakfast with a patient mum who allowed time for dressing and doing up buttons and zips! Nevertheless, in every home there would be some sequence of events that children could rely on and recall in conversation. The common practice of starting the nursery day informally allows children to join in at their own pace—some need a quiet time after the early morning hustle, while others are bursting with physical energy.

Milk time

This is often left to children to decide themselves, but even then an individual routine can be suggested.

> Would you like to have your milk when you've finished your painting?

When milk is served more formally, there are signs of getting it ready—one or two tables need to be cleared of toys, games and dolls, so that table-mats and chairs may be arranged—and there is a clearing away afterwards. This is often a signal for a change in the activities offered.

> After milk time we will go for a walk to see the trains.

Clearing-up time

This is an important part of the daily routine as it provides a very real time clue and an idea of sequence, as packing away toys comes after the time for playing with them, but before the time for lunch, etc. When there is only one teacher, the usual practice is to give a five minute warning, so that children have a chance to "finish off". This sometimes leads children to start on something new, in the belief that five minutes is a "long long time". When children are playing in groups with adults, clearing up is the natural end to an activity, and can always be linked to the next.

> When we have packed away the blocks we can put out the mats ready for a story.

Story time

Most children look forward to story time because they enjoy a feeling of closeness with an adult. To build up this rapport between an adult and group of children, outside interruptions should be kept to a minimum. For this reason, the end of the session is probably not the best regular time for a story, and "after Miss B. has had her coffee" may be much more convenient. In this way children begin to establish points in time which help them to understand its passing.

Providing this uninterrupted regular time can be preserved, even the noisiest, most active child can be helped to anticipate and enjoy the five or ten minutes of quiet listening, with his own special adult, although some of his friends may still be playing in another part of the room.

"It's time for our story."

Of course, a story may occur spontaneously during some other activity in order to augment or illustrate a particular point. Then, questions such as "Do we have time?" or, "Would you like to have your milk later, so that you can hear it?" and statements like "It's a long one" help the children to gauge the time needed.

The length of story is chosen to fit the maturity of the children or the time available. Remarks, such as "that was a long story", help us to gauge their span of concentration.

Always, there can be a lead in to the next part of the routine. It may be time to wash hands and prepare for dinner, enjoy painting, creative work, or to look for coats and prepare for home.

Meal times

When children have their midday meal at school, it may be possible to link this with home and family routines.

> Do dad/mum have dinner in the evening when they come home from work?
> Is lunch different from breakfast and tea? How? What food do we eat at breakfast time?
> Do you all have dinner together on Saturday and Sunday?

Questions like this will lead to many unexpected answers, but may begin to establish that meals usually occur at certain intervals with a gap between for doing other things.

Rest time

In some schools, rest is given to pupils who need it in a more or less organised manner. In these cases, children come to realise that putting away beds and blankets comes after the rest but before the next time for painting or other activities. It may seem a very long rest time if the child feels he does not really need it.

Home time

For many children, especially when they first start at school, this is the time for which they have been waiting. Events such as clearing up, finishing off, and, quite often, rhymes, etc., herald the parents' arrival. This gives an opportunity for sequencing events. Also, words such as "Your mummy is early, John" or, "Mummy will be late, Jacky" help to instil time notions in children. A lot of ordinal number work can be done—"Whose mum was first?", "Who went home third?" and so on.

As they mature, children begin to gauge the span of a day by asking questions such as "Have we had our dinner?", "Is it afternoon yet?" They may think that they should be at home and in bed as the daylight hours become less in the autumn and they go home in the twilight.

At this age, a child's concept of a day is that part of the 24 hours when it is light and he is not in bed. "All day" to him means from waking until going to bed and not the 9 a.m. to 3.30 p.m. he is at the school. We must be prepared to count in days and nights for him, so that at a later stage, 24 hours can be accepted as one day and the 24 hour clock understood.

The weekly routine

Names of days

Some children come to school able to recite the days of the week, but they need some practical activity with which to connect them. It is often convenient for teachers and their helpers to have a set routine for certain activities and although this should be flexible, it can help a child to see a sequence and pattern of events if he can tie these activities to a particular day. There may be visits by students, parents or other adults, outings to places of interest or just the regular day by day activities of the class. It is not suggested that *every* day must have a linked activity, but that the teacher might take advantage of those that do.

Monday is often connected with bringing dinner-money or pennies for apples. But without any money reference, it is often a special day, the day to introduce a new activity, to refill empty flower vases, or to begin to set up a new display table for colour, texture or size.

Tuesday may be the day to watch a special TV programme or use the large apparatus in a school hall.

Wednesday could be a washing day—dolls' clothes one week, sheets and pillow cases another week.

Thursday may be a day to clean pets' cages, renewing sawdust, hay, etc., in addition to the daily attentions.

Friday, as the last day of the school week, is another special day. Toys and apparatus may need to be packed away more securely, tablecloths and table-mats need a "proper wash". A special activity may need to be finished off before interest is lost during the weekend break.

Saturday and *Sunday* can be discussed as the days when children do things with their parents and relations, e.g. "Daddy always works on his car on Sundays." "We go to Auntie's house on Saturdays." Children may paint pictures of their weekend outings.

Past and future

While keeping to a pre-set plan as far as practicable, flexibility is necessary. If the guinea pig's cage gets extra dirty, it may be suggested to give it a good clean today, instead of waiting till tomorrow for the right day! Or if it rains on the morning it was decided to walk to the shops, that expedition can "wait until tomorrow". A TV programme seen yesterday may be discussed, as well as the various days and activities that will happen before the next one.

Children and their parents often devise their own ways of counting days. It can be "two more sleeps" before we go to the beach, or "after rubbish-collection day". At this stage children seem more ready to talk about tomorrow and predict into the future than to recall what happened yesterday or last week.

Vocabulary: today – tomorrow – yesterday – week – next week – last week – the day before yesterday – the day after tomorrow – last night – days of the week.

Longer periods of time

The seasons

Many pictures, wall charts and children's books try to

convey impressions of the seasons and have illustrations of children dressed suitably, e.g. scarf and gloves portray winter while bathing costumes mean summer. Although these may be good starting points for conversation, it is doubtful whether very young children see the significance, or even remember a previous season. The first misty day of the autumn may be a chance to say, "Who remembers another day like this?" Children can watch for breaks in the mist, decide what they can see from the window and try to recall what they usually see. Very hot days, snowy or frosty days can all receive special treatment and a group may enjoy keeping a simple pictorial weather record. A run of sunny hot days might signify that it is summer, or in the winter they could mark up the days when there is snow or frost to be seen. (For other ideas, see Parry, M. and Archer, H. *Two to Five*, p. 43, Macmillan, 1975.)

The clothes that the children are wearing can be discussed to lead towards awareness of the changes of the seasons. In the autumn, colour changes of leaves, fading of flowers and the shorter hours of daylight can all be brought to the notice of the children and they may remember some of them when the next autumn comes around. Spring-time can be celebrated in the same way—looking for the first green leaves on the trees or flowers in the garden can be really exciting for a three-year-old who can only remember bare branches and earth. If bulbs are planted in the autumn, it may be worth digging one or two up while they are flowering, so that children who are curious can be shown that the flowers have come from the original bulbs. It is not sufficient for the children to see only bulbs growing in bottles as, at their age, they are generally unable to transfer what they see happening in one growing medium to the other. To have bulbs growing in both media is probably the best solution.

Example

Vanessa (4.4) was playing with the clay: "This is the little garden and it is dying. All the leaves are coming off the trees and when it's spring-time again all the leaves will come again—new leaves. There's just this one apple left on this tree."

"There's just this one apple left on this tree."

Festivals and holidays

The preparation for an enjoyment of various festivals during the year (such as Christmas, Easter, May Day and local celebrations) give the children some idea of continuity. As they take part, they are likely to remember the highlights, good or bad, of the year before, and their memory begins to develop.

A holiday from school, especially during the summer, is often a much longer period than the family holiday spent away from home. (In fact, many children do not have such a family holiday.) Very young children cannot foresee such a span of time, but when they are involved in the arrangements to be made for the care of pets and watering of plants, they are sure to realise that the last days before a holiday are not just ordinary days. When they return to the classroom, questions such as, "How much have I grown?" and "How much taller than me has the sunflower grown?" help to establish this longer period of time and also that events continue to happen in the classroom although the children are not there themselves.

Vocabulary: winter – spring – summer – autumn – year – month – this year – last year – next year.

Birthdays and How old am I?

How old am I?

Many children can answer the question "How old are you?", but if the next question is "four what?" or "How many birthdays have you had before?", the children's very limited knowledge is revealed. Sizes and ages are often confused and while the four-year-old can expect to be bigger than his two-year-old brother, he may also be bigger than all the other four-year-olds in the nursery, prompting such remarks as, "I am bigger than John, so I must have more candles on my birthday cake".

Birthdays are celebrated in many different ways; there may be parties at school, at home and at a relative's house, so that the celebrations become more important than the actual date of the birthday, and children are confused into thinking that they have several each year. There is even the possibility of thinking that the night between being four-years-old and five-years-old must be a year. The following ideas may be of help.

A collection of photographs showing individual children from a few days old up to their present age may help to show the way they have altered.

A collection of magazine pictures may be sorted into babies, children, teenagers, grown-ups and grandparents.

In their imaginative play, children pretend to be babies, as well as parents and grandparents. Dolls and tiny doll's house people are often given specific ages.

When listening to stories and rhymes children will readily imitate "old men", babies or ladies, e.g. "This is the way the ladies ride . . ." The "props" used in this play can emphasise different ages. Stories from teachers, parents and grandparents about "when I was young" give more ideas of continuity and growing up.

Will I catch up?

Children gradually associate ages of themselves and others with social and educational stages such as going to the swimming pool, staying out late, going to the "very big school" by bus, leaving school and starting work. Adults who say that these pleasures are only for "big" boys and girls, help to confuse the young child's thoughts about age and size, and it is more helpful to talk about getting older. Conversation about younger brothers and sisters can include: "She can crawl and walk because she is nearly two and she has had one birthday." "I can come to the class because I'm three." "When you are nearly five, you go to the big school."

Looking at adults around him, the young child has no idea of their actual age, although he often thinks that the most important one is the oldest. On the other hand, he sees the tallest adult as the oldest and cannot believe that a short person can be older than the others. With this sort of confusion, young children are sure to think that they will catch up with their elders, and in saying "When I'm as old as you" they really believe they will "catch up", as this conversation with some children shows.

Example

Tracey: Mrs. R., when I grow up I'm going to work for you!

Clare: So will I. We'll tidy for you!

Teacher: That will be nice, but won't I have to wait a long, long time?

Clare: Yes—until we are six.

Tracey: No, we won't be grown up until we are ten and that will be longer.

Again, the sequence of events that must happen between leaving the kindergarten atmosphere and joining the adult world can be introduced, referring perhaps to older brothers and sisters who are at various other schools.

Some teachers have tried various ways to help children see that there is a sequence to events, and some of the ideas given below may be useful.

Children can sort a bundle of pictures which illustrate a favourite story and try to put them in the right order.

Pets that are brought into the classroom as babies will change in appearance and size as they grow older, and children can watch for these differences.

Example
Elliott (4.3) was waiting anxiously for frog spawn to change into frogs.
Elliott: They haven't changed yet.
The teacher explained that it took a long time, about two weeks, for them to develop into tadpoles and then a long time before they grew into frogs. She explained that Elliott had been a baby and it took a long time for him to grow into a boy and it would be even longer before he grew into a man, and it was the same with tadpoles—they took a long time to grow into frogs.

Elliott seemed satisfied. He went away and several minutes later came back and asked, "Will they have changed when we've had our dinner and our pudding?"

This teacher has done her best to explain, but it is obvious that Elliott has a long way to go before he begins to understand.

Piaget (Piaget, Jean, *The Child's Conception of Time*, Chapter 9, Parts 1, 2 and 3, Routledge & Kegan Paul, 1969) has written about many experiments with children of four years and upwards as they explore the problem of age. He shows how the younger ones continually use size as synonymous with age and see no connection between being born first and remaining the oldest. Questions he put about trees and animals led young children to make clear distinctions between grown-up and old or young, without understanding that the fully grown-up man, animal or plant continued to grow older.

Vocabulary: old – older – young – younger – age – grown-up.

How long does it take?

Overlap of activity
The previous sections have dealt mainly with helping children to establish fixed points in time rather than measuring its passing. Most young children do not see an activity as having a beginning and end or realise that different activities can overlap or happen at the same time.

Seeing his mother prepare a stew for lunch, a child may assume that mother has spent all the morning cooking, not understanding that whilst the cooking is going on, shopping, cleaning and washing may also be happening.

If a few children leave the classroom for a short expedition or just to do some cooking in another room, they are usually surprised to find that although they have missed all the usual activities, other children have been doing them and it is already time for dinner. They expect to find everything as they left it, not realising that events unconnected with themselves continue. So, going to the park can take a whole morning and may be referred to as such before setting out—We will go down the road, over the bridge, into the park and play on the swings. While we are away, Mrs A. will be cooking our dinner, so that it's ready for us when we get back.

How much can I do?
Egg timers, water clocks, pingers and some of the commercially-made timers are fascinating to children of all

ages. Young children will also enjoy helping to improvise timers such as:

a large bucket suspended over a bowl trickling sand or water through a small hole;

a small candle burning right down or a larger one burning to a mark;

improvised "egg timers" made from two plastic containers joined at their narrow necks and containing sand—try both wet and dry.

The passage of time can also be observed when:

noticing movement of shadows on sunny days;

painting a patch of concrete with plain water on a hot sunny day and waiting for it to dry, or after rain, waiting for the playground to dry.

Games may be organised to see what can be done in a given time and estimations made. These games should not be made into races. The aim is to do the job properly and then see if you beat the timer.

Can we put all the outdoor toys away before the concrete dries?

Shall we all try to button our coats before the sand runs through?

"I can do up all my buttons before it runs through!"

What is five minutes?

As children become familiar with these simple ways of measuring the passing of time, names can be introduced for them, for example, five minutes for the sand to run through the bucket and to pack the bricks away; or ten minutes to lay the tables for lunch.

Most adults learn to gauge the amount that can be accomplished in a given time, and will say to a child, "There's not time to paint a picture before dinner" or "You have time to do that puzzle before we clear up". Gradually children come to ask similar questions, as they compare the activities they can accomplish in a given time. "Is there time to get dressed and play in the sand pit before story time?" "Can I paint a picture before mummy comes?"

Faster and slower

Young children like to compare the speed at which they can do things.

I can run down the hill faster than you.

It takes you longer to run down the hill than me.

They also begin to realise that they can control the time taken by their own actions; crawling slowly, for example, or running quickly.

I can put those away quicker than you.

Example

A class of four-year-olds were using the water wheel in the water trough or sand tray.

Mark: I can make it go fast.

Teacher: How can you make it go more slowly?

Mary: Use a little funnel.

Tony: Use a bottle with a little hole.

Angela: Pour the water more slowly.

Vocabulary: hours – minutes – long time – short time.

Stories, rhymes and music

The youngest children accept stories as present-day facts, but gradually as their experience widens they will recognise the "Once upon a time" beginning and at a later stage still will ask "Is it true?" When an adult says that something happened a long, long time ago, he understands what is meant, but time is relative and the interval between lunch and tea may seem a very long time to a three-year-old.

Stories about our own or the children's grandparents begin to give the children ideas about "long ago". How did people travel about before there were so many cars and buses? Very young children cannot be expected to differentiate between pre-historic, biblical and modern times, and to the three-year-old "long ago" could mean only yesterday.

There are many rhymes and games where clocks and time are mentioned and children become familiar with the vocabulary. (See the second part of this booklet.)

Most young children readily respond to music on piano, guitar, percussion, improvised instruments and records. They will clap, tap and bang out rhythms, and once they have learnt to listen, begin to differentiate between fast and slow beats, gradually fitting their own body movements to the rhythms. There are many informal opportunities to participate in the "music corner" as well as the more formal movement session.

Clock time

Children come into contact with clocks in many different ways, on the street, at home, on TV, looking at dad's watch. Some children learn to tell the time at home at a very early age, while others seem to find it very difficult. A simple clock face, with hands that can be set, will lead to many matching activities.

a) When cooking, the clock face can be set at the time for removing the biscuits from the oven and the real clock watched until it matches. If the time involved is from 10 until 10.15 for example, it could be suggested that the washing up could be done in that time, and "fifteen minutes" then becomes another time span. Later the children could be asked, "Do you remember that we did all the washing up while the biscuits were being cooked? What else could we do in the same time?"

Note that there is no suggestion here that the children should be able to recognise the numeral "15" or have any idea of its symbolism. We are simply giving a name to another period of time.

b) Gradually other periods of time can be introduced and related to the movement of the hands of the clock, so that older children are ready to learn to tell the time with understanding.

Before actually learning to tell the time, such matching activities will lead children to recognise the position of the hands on different clocks and identify them with times that are significant to them: nine o'clock to come to school; five o'clock for TV; half past seven for bedtime.

Example
This four-year-old shows her stage of understanding.
Joanne (4.4), walking around the paths in the playground, stopped as she passed the teacher.
Joanne: I'm taking my children to school. (Next time around, looking at her wrist and pointing) My watch says it's ten o'clock. I should have been there by now. (Runs off)

Vocabulary: hours – minutes – long time – short time.

The teacher's role

Many teachers feel that the social and emotional needs of very young children must come before any attempt to promote intellectual growth. But in the very act of providing a regular caring relationship with them, teachers are helping children to come to terms with the world around them. The concept of time will be assimilated very slowly right through to adulthood. But if some of the ideas suggested are put into practice, children will begin to see their part in the general pattern of days, weeks, months and years. By listening to their conversation, we can recognise their attempts to understand the passing of time.

A conversation, like the one that follows, shows just how confused a child can be.

Example 1
At a pastry table in Home Corner, Karen (4.7) had been making an apple pie.

Karen: There, it's baking now.
Teacher: It's a big pie. Will it take long?
Karen: A long many times. (Looks at calendar on house wall) Twenty-four—it'll take that many.

She knows that a pie takes a long time to cook, but has no other way of expressing it. Trying to please, she mixes calendar and clock times, leaving her teacher with a very good opportunity to follow up either.

Example 2
David (3.10) commenting on autumn leaves: "Those used to be on the trees in the summer."

This remark could start a conversation on growth and activities such as going out to look at trees whose leaves had not yet fallen, looking for buds on the bare branches that will lead to next year's leaves and thus putting autumn into its place in the year.

The next examples show teachers leading on the conversation, helping children to think and express themselves logically.

Example 3
Paul (3.9) was helping to put bricks away.
Paul: Is it nearly mummy time?
Teacher: Yes. How do you know?
Paul: We always clear the bricks away when it's nearly mummy time.

Example 4
Abigail (4.10):   I'm going to Looe not today, not tomorrow, not the next day but the day after that. [i.e. Saturday.]
On Friday the teacher asked her when she was going to Looe.
Abigail: Tomorrow.
Teacher: Last time you told me you had to wait a few days.
Abigail: Yes, but it's sooner now.

Example 5
Deborah (4.3):   She's locked in jail.
Adult: Oh, why is she locked in jail?
Beverley (4.10): Because she opened her present.
Adult: That's a funny reason for locking her in jail. Is she going to be there long?
Deborah: A long long long time.
Beverley: Right up to dinner time.
Adult: Is dinner time a long long time?
Beverley: Yes. The big ones are out to play—then we have dance—then we have story—then we have to wash—then dinner—a long long long time.
Deborah: We go out to play before we wash so it is a long long long long long long time. [The length of time to dinner was $1\frac{1}{4}$ hours approximately.]

It is unlikely that any great progression will be seen in children's ideas about time at this early stage. But from understanding short times such as "before dinner" and "after story-time" they may go on to seeing that Monday comes after the weekend and that seeds have to be planted before they begin to grow. From repeating such phrases as "in a minute" with no meaning, they begin to say that the biscuits will take twenty minutes to cook and have some idea of how long this will be. As well as predicting what will happen tomorrow, more mature children will remember and recount what happened yesterday, distinguishing it from events of last week or last year. Verbal clock times such as "twelve o'clock is dinner time" will gradually be matched with the pattern on the clock face until the children can predict the activity by watching the clock face. Later, they learn to "tell the time" and relate these words and clock-face patterns to their past experience.

12 Rhymes and Stories

Introduction

> Walking round the garden
> Like a teddy bear,
> One step, two steps . . .
> Tickling under there

The toddler shrieks with anticipation and delight at the tickling session that follows. Jingles and rhymes are an integral part of our tradition and often start at mother's or grandmother's knee, even before the baby can talk or walk. The child obviously experiences pleasure, at being the centre of attention, but does he actually learn anything from these rhymes? Certainly we do not expect the toddler to be able to count "one", "two", having heard the words, but he may well be able to join in with the recitation after a while.

The child will encounter many rhymes and stories which involve mathematical ideas—sometimes quite explicitly, sometimes hidden by more obvious notions. Few would claim that a child will gain a mathematical concept simply by learning rhymes and listening to stories. However, such experiences, when linked to others, will help to accumulate the knowledge leading to a firm understanding of the concept. It is in this context, without expecting too much of any one particular rhyme or story, that this guide can claim relevance.

Of course, there is a danger that mathematics will be "forced" into all rhymes and stories. Teachers should beware of this, but equally, they should be aware of the mathematics which can arise *should the opportunity be ripe*.

Example
Children are often exposed to the old favourite:

> One, two, three, four, five,
> Once I caught a fish alive
> Six, seven, eight, nine, ten,
> Then I let it go again.
> Why did you let it go?
> Because it bit my finger so.
> Which finger did it bite?
> This little finger on the right.

The mathematical content of this rhyme and its usefulness in the development of ideas can be seen easily. Just counting, one, two, three, four, five, can become an early experience in matching, by getting the children to hold up their fingers to match, or for one child to pick out, one at a time, five children, or even four other children to join him. Ideas of right and left begin to form as the right hand is indicated as the one that was bitten, and, of course, also arise with gloves, shoes, buttons on coats and in general conversation. In themselves, these experiences are slight and fleeting but added to many others, in an enjoyable atmosphere, they may well begin to have some effect. Certainly the child will take pleasure and pride in repeating rhymes at home, as most young children enjoy their "party pieces", but there is more to it than this.

Possible developments

Rhymes

There are many rhymes, some of which are set to music, which involve numbers. Some are counting rhymes, others begin addition and subtraction.

Counting up to five

> One, two, three,
> Mother caught a flea,
> Put it in the teapot,
> And made a cup of tea.
> The flea jumped out,
> Mother gave a shout,
> And father came in
> With his shirt hanging out!

*   *   *

"Hickory Dickory Dock" is an old favourite. The children clap the appropriate number of times when "the clock strikes" and use their hands for the swinging pendulum. Activities which may lead up to or from this rhyme include a study of the time at which things happen, making pictures of clocks or models in clay, etc.

Example

Dittony (4.5):   Does the pendulum go tick-tock?
Sally-Ann (4.4):   Does the clock stand on the floor?
Dittony: Stretch the clock to make it fit and press it to the wall.
Ann (4.0):   Put whiskers on the mouse.

*   *   *

> Here's a ball,
> And here's a ball,
> And a great big ball I see.
> Shall we count them?
> Are you ready?
> One, two, three.

As with many other rhymes, the value of this one is that it is easy to illustrate, preferably with real balls, but even with circular shapes of various sizes. Discussions of size and shape can proceed.

*   *   *

> Stepping over stepping stones, one, two, three,
> Stepping over stepping stones, come with me!
> The river's very fast
> And the river's very wide
> And we'll step across on stepping stones
> And reach the other side.

*   *   *

> When Goldilocks went to the house of the bears
> Oh what did her blue eyes see?
> A bowl that was huge
> A bowl that was small
> A bowl that was tiny and that was all.
> She counted them one, two, three.

When Goldilocks went to the house of the bears
Oh what did her blue eyes see?
A chair that was huge
A chair that was small
A chair that was tiny and that was all.
She counted them one, two, three.

When Goldilocks went to the house of the bears
Oh what did her blue eyes see?
A bed that was huge, etc.

When Goldilocks went to the house of the bears
Oh what did her blue eyes see?
A bear that was huge, etc.

This is a great favourite which is usually sung and accompanied by suitable actions. This not only brings in counting but suggests ordering and comparisons of size.

*   *   *

Every morning at eight o'clock
You can hear the postman's knock.
Up jumps Mary to open the door
One letter, two letters, three letters, four.

This is an action rhyme which can lead to notions of distance, costs, size of letters, etc.

Here is the beehive, where are the bees?
Hidden away where nobody sees.
Soon they come creeping out of the hive,
One, two, three, four, five.

One can build a "beehive" from a box and put five "bees" inside. Flannelgraphs or fingers can also be used.

Peter taps with one hammer,
One hammer, one hammer,
Peter taps with one hammer
This fine day.
    (tap, tap, tap)

Peter taps with two hammers, etc.
Peter taps with three hammers, etc.
Peter taps with four hammers, etc.
Peter taps with five hammers, etc.

Peter goes to sleep now
    (lay head on hands)
Sleep now, sleep now,
Peter goes to sleep now,
This fine day.

This can be a very useful singing game. Use one hand for the first hammer, then both hands, both hands and one foot, both hands and both feet, and, finally, all this plus a nodding head.

This can help with one-to-one correspondence. How many taps do we have after each verse?

*   *   *

One little, two little, three little witches
Flying over haystacks, flying over ditches,
Sliding down the moonbeam without any hitches,
Hi, ho, Hallowe'en's here.

*   *   *

These next three rhymes can help introduce the idea of ordinal number.

Five little snowmen, happy and gay,
The first one said, "What a beautiful day."
The second one said, "We'll never have tears."
The third one said, "We'll stay here for years."
The fourth one said, "But what will happen in May?"
The fifth one said, "Look! We're melting away!"

Watch my hens and you will see,
They walk always one, two, three.
First the black one leads the line,
Next the white with feathers fine.
Brownie follows last and she
Makes the third one you will see.

Five little squirrels sitting on a tree
The first one said "What can I see?"
The next [second] one said "A man with a gun."
The next [third] one said "Let's run, let's run."
The next [fourth] one said "Let's hide in the shade."
The next [fifth] one said "Why? I'm not afraid."
But BANG went the gun and they all ran away.

* * *

The old favourite "Hot Cross Buns" also falls into this category of rhymes.

The number concept

Many rhymes provide excellent reference sets for some numbers. These can be used to build up the child's notion of a number.

I can knock with my two hands, knock, knock, knock!
I can rock with my two hands, rock, rock, rock!
I can tap with my two hands, tap, tap, tap!
I can clap with my two hands, clap, clap, clap!

* * *

Two fat gentlemen met in a lane
Bowed most politely, bowed once again.
How do you do?
How do you do?
And how do you do again?

Two thin ladies met in a lane, etc.

Two tall policemen met in a lane, etc.
Two little schoolboys met in a lane, etc.
Two tiny babies met in a lane, etc.

This delightful finger play can lead to modelling, flannelgraphs, drawings. Discussions on size may follow.

* * *

Five little peas in a pea-pod pressed
(Clench fingers on one hand)
One grew, two grew and so did all the rest.
(Raise fingers slowly)
They grew and grew and did not stop
Until one day the pod went "pop".
(Clap loudly)

This is an action rhyme which could come after a gardening discussion or a visit to a greengrocer's

* * *

Three red plums on the old plum tree,
One for you and one for me
And one for the boy who picks them.

Draw or model a plum tree and set out the rhyme. This can be combined with many other notions of "threeness".

* * *

Some of the traditional rhymes can also be used in this context. For example:

Two Little Dicky-Birds   Rub-a-dub-dub
Three Blind Mice   Baa Baa Black Sheep

Example
Teacher: How many bags of wool did the black
                sheep have?
Joanne (3.6):   Three bags. That is how old I am.
Teacher: Is there a lot of wool in each bag?

Joanne:	Yes, they are full.
Teacher:	How do you know?
Joanne:	Because it tells you in the story. Full means a lot.

More counting rhymes

Here we have rhymes which can be used in more complicated counting settings—counting backwards, counting by twos, threes, etc., and counting to numbers larger than five. Some of these rhymes will be inappropriate for many nursery children, but in each class there may be one or two children who could use some extra mathematical stimulation.

Counting backwards
　　Two little blackbirds singing in the sun,
　　One flew away and then there was one.
　　One little blackbird, very black and small,
　　He flew away and then there was the wall.
　　One little brick wall lonely in the rain,
　　Waiting for the blackbirds to come and sing again.

Use fingers for the birds and folded arms for the wall.

*　　*　　*

　　Five little seeds a-sleeping they lay
　　A-sleeping they lay.
　　A bird flew down and took one away.
　　How many seeds were left that day?
　　Four little seeds, etc.

If appropriate, this rhyme can be continued until there are no seeds present.

Five children curl up on the floor. The child who is the bird stands on chair with arms outstretched, jumps down and takes one "seed" away. When all the seeds have been taken, the rest of the group "blow" all the seeds back again. Real seeds (e.g. acorns) can be used with a child taking one away at the appropriate time.

*　　*　　*

　　Five little froggies sitting on a well
　　One looked up and in he fell.
　　Froggies jumped high,
　　Froggies jumped low;
　　Four little froggies dancing to and fro, etc.

Use fingers to represent frogs, and reduce the number held up for each verse. Wiggle fingers to represent the actions of the frogs.

*　　*　　*

　　Five little monkeys walked along the shore,
　　One went a-sailing, then there were four.

　　Four little monkeys climbed up a tree,
　　One of them tumbled down, then there were three.

　　Three little monkeys found a pot of glue,
　　One got stuck in it, then there were two.

　　Two little monkeys found a currant bun,
　　One ran away with it, then there was one.

　　One little monkey cried all afternoon,
　　He was put into an aeroplane, and sent to the moon.

There are lots of actions here. Other animals can be substituted.

*　　*　　*

Other favourites, some of which could be used to introduce zero, are:

Five Little Ducks	Ten Green Bottles
Five Currant Buns	Ten Little Indians
	There Were Ten in the Bed

Example

Martin (4.2):	(After singing 'Ten Green Bottles'.) Mine haven't broken; I've got two left.
Teacher:	Why?
Martin:	They didn't fall off because they've got flat bottoms.
Teacher:	What do you mean by that?
Martin:	Smooth. They didn't wobble over.

Counting in twos or more

> One big tanker goes rolling by
> How many big wheels can you spy?
> Two big tankers . . .

Take this one as far as the children care to go. A model of a tanker may help. The rhyme can lead to all sorts of questions about transport, oil, etc.

*　　*　　*

> Ten galloping horses galloping through the town,
> Five were white and five were brown,
> Five galloped up and five galloped down,
> Ten galloping horses galloping through the town.

*　　*　　*

> Five little ladies going for a walk,
> (walk fingers of left hand)
> Five little ladies stopped for a talk,
> (tap left hand finger tips on table)
> Along came five little gentlemen
> (walk fingers of right hand towards others)
> They all danced together and that made ten.
> (dance fingers together)

Other examples include:

Hickety, Pickety, My Black Hen
As I Was Going to St. Ives　　Two, Four, Six, Eight

Counting beyond five

> One, two, three, four, five, six, seven,
> All good children go to heaven.

*　　*　　*

One, two, three, four, Mary at the cottage door,
Five, six, seven, eight, eating cherries off a plate.

*　　*　　*

One potato, two potatoes, three potatoes, four,
Five potatoes, six potatoes, seven potatoes, more.
OUT spells out.

This rhyme could be introduced after a session of potato printing, or a visit to the greengrocer's.

*　　*　　*

Other possibilities are:

One, Two, Buckle my Shoe	One Man Went to Mow
The Twelve Days of Christmas	One Little Brown Bird
This Old Man	Sing a Song of Sixpence
Pease Porridge Hot	

Space and shape

Many rhymes involve notions of size, shape, direction and position. (One favourite example is "The Grand Old Duke of York".) These can be used to introduce such notions or help to consolidate them in the child's mind. A great amount of movement can be introduced into some of the following rhymes.

*　　*　　*

> When I was one year old
> (hold up one finger)
> I was very very small,
> (hold two hands slightly apart)

But now I'm (three . . .) years old
    (hold up number of fingers)
I'm growing big and tall.
    (put hand over top of head)

*   *   *

A tree looks really very tall
To me because I'm small,
But if I see a little mouse
Then I am taller than his house.
So what is small
And what is tall?
Let's see what we can find . . .

A good introduction to the ideas of comparison. See chapter 2 *Comparisons* for further activities.

*   *   *

Curl round small
Like a little mouse.
Stretch up tall
As high as a house.
Now pretend you have a drum
Beat like this rum, tum, tum.
Shake your fingers,
Stamp your feet,
Close eyes tightly and go to sleep.

*   *   *

Here we go up, up, up
Here we go down, down, down
Here we go backwards and forwards
And here we go round and round.

This is an action rhyme with lots of movement. It could be carried out on a set of steps.

Open, shut them, open, shut them,
Give a little clap.
Open, shut them, open, shut them,
Lay them in your lap.
Creep them, creep them, creep them, creep them
Right up to your chin,
Open wide your little mouth
But do not let them in.
Roll them, roll them, roll them, roll them
To your lap like this,
Shake them, shake them, shake them, shake them
Then blow a little kiss.

*   *   *

I am a bouncing, bouncing ball!
I bounce over hedges and ditches and all
I bounce up high and I bounce down low
The harder you bounce me, the higher I go.

As well as maths here, we also have the beginnings for scientific experiment.

*   *   *

Here is a crocodile crawling through the mud,
Crawling, crawling, crawling through the mud.

Here is a kangaroo hopping over the hill,
Hopping, hopping, hopping over the hill.

Here is a polar bear climbing up the rocks . . .

Here is a penguin waddling on the path . . .

Here is a koala bear climbing down the tree . . .

Many "space" words are included in this rhyme. The animals mentioned are also worthy of study.

The passage of time

Time is a difficult concept for children to grasp. Some of the rhymes below may help.

*   *   *

Morning is for waking up
And getting out of bed
Afternoon is tea-time
And after that it's bed.

The sequence of time-linked events is brought out here. Pictures could be drawn by the children and put in order of events.

*   *   *

When the big hand points straight up
The little hand tells the time.
It's . . o'clock, it's . . o'clock (leader says numbers 1–12)
Listen for the chime.
(Children clap appropriate number of times.)

*   *   *

Other possibilities are:

Wee Willie Winkie   Cobbler Cobbler
Hickory Dickory Dock   January Brings the Snow

Games

Many rhymes have well established games associated with them. These include old favourites such as: Ring-a-ring-o-roses; In and out the dusky bluebells; In and out the windows; Farmer's in his den; Here we go Looby-loo; The big ship sails; Oranges and lemons; Here we go round the mulberry bush.

All of these, and many others, give children the opportunity to link actions with words. This, in itself, is an experience in matching, while many other mathematical ideas are contained in the actual words and movements. Thus, a child can be "the last, last, last man in" or can be asked to "put your left foot in, your left foot out" and so on. Playing games such as these also allows sequencing activities to be experienced. For example, in "Farmer's in his den" the characters are assembled in a certain order. In "What's the time Mr. Wolf?" the suspense can be built up by using the hours leading up to the children's own dinner time. Some games involve "taking turns"—an experience which is desirable both mathematically and socially.

Many of the rhymes listed in the previous sections can be used as games. One good example is "Peter Hammers". More can be found in *This Little Puffin* (Matterson, Elizabeth M., Ed., *This little Puffin—Finger Play and Nursery Games*, Puffin Books, Penguin, 1969). A full list of song books for young children may be obtained from the British Association for Early Childhood Education, Montgomery Hall, The Oval, London SE11 5SW.

Stories

Story telling can be a great delight to all concerned and no one would wish to diminish the pleasure and security of the occasion by interrupting a story with some mathematical notion. Nevertheless, mathematics can arise quite naturally in some stories and can be pinpointed after the story telling when repetition and discussion take place; such remarks as "what happened first and then what happened next?"; "What did the second little pig decide to build his house from?"; "Which billy goat gruff was the biggest?"; "How many bowls of porridge did Goldilocks find?". These and many other starting points help to sow the seeds of mathematical notions such as sequence, ordering, comparisons, matching and, of course, counting.

Many old favourites can be used to lead into mathematical activities. Sometimes it is not even necessary to read the whole story but to simply have the children recall the important points. However, it should again be stressed that the mathematics should not crowd out the enjoyment of a story. Some favourites which lead into various mathematical notions are:

The Old Woman and her Pig	The Little Red Hen
The Three Little Pigs	Epaminandas
The Gingerbread Boy	The Snowy Day
The Three Billy Goats Gruff	Whistle for Willy
Henny Penny	The Tale of the Turnip

The Old Woman who Lived in a Vinegar Bottle
The Miller, his Son and their Donkey
The Woman who Always Argued

Teachers will doubtless add their own favourites to this list. See the next section for some examples of conversations which followed story telling.

In order to give some idea as to mathematics which can arise from a story, consider the tale of "The Elves and the Shoemaker". Again, it should be made quite clear that the aim of this guide is *not* to suggest where you may interrupt such a story in order to delve into its mathematical side. Some questions which could bring out mathematics in this story include:

What is a *pair*? (as in pair of shoes). Lead on to other things which come in pairs including socks, trousers, gloves . . .
The shoemaker cuts out the leather for the shoes before he goes to bed. This could lead to much discussion about bedtimes, rising times, other times . . .
Why didn't the shoemaker make the shoes straight after he cut out the leather? This could lead to ideas of enough time, too little time . . . Once the lead

has been made other activities can be carried through.

The doubling of the number of pairs of shoes each night and the paying of twice the normal price for each pair provides the opportunity for other "doubling" rhymes (e.g. Two, Four, Six, Eight) to be introduced. This can lead to other doubling activities and to a stronger notion of the number two.

The elves in the story could provide the impetus for a great deal of work on comparison of size. For example, comparison of shoes, clothes, heights, etc. can be made. Make models of furniture, houses, cars, towns, etc. for elves.
There are many "position" and "time" ideas which can be derived from the story, including: evening, morning, last, tomorrow, next, early, corner of the room, behind, midnight, quickly.

Of course, no teacher would try to bring out all these ideas at one sitting. The real value is as a back-up to something previously introduced, as a consolidation for something previously learned, or as a stimulus towards some new idea. *Do not follow every story with some mathematical appendix, but be aware of the possibilities.*

Teachers often make up their own stories about the children. The stories should be simple and involve many references to the children/child. Some notions which might be mentioned are:
The Child: Age, size—whether short, medium height or tall; hair long, short, colour; clothing; favourite times, birthdays, Christmas, Festivals, holidays, television time.
Background of child: Family—number and ages of brothers/sisters. Has the child travelled—overseas from country to city or vice versa.
Environment: Streets—narrow or wide; straight or winding; buildings—tall with long shadows, old/new, bungalows.

The teacher's role

As has already been mentioned, rhymes and stories have an intrinsic value which does not depend on their mathematical content. The pleasure experienced by a child who hears a story, joins in the words and actions of a rhyme, or dances in a singing game should not be disturbed by the over-zealous teacher searching for facts. The chance does arise sometimes, however, to involve the child in some mathematical experience derived from this pleasure, perhaps a painting, some model building or another rhyme. More usually, however, a rhyme or story will be just one experience among many which help develop certain concepts.

The following example is given at length to show how one teacher exploited a rhyme in many directions, the mathematics falling in naturally among many other activities.

Example 1
A child brought a mobile of ladybirds and daisies to school. The children then found ladybirds in the garden. The rhyme was introduced:

> Ladybird, ladybird, fly away home,
> Your house is on fire your children all gone.

This led to the following activities.

Painting
The children painted ladybirds and these were used as a frieze. The colours used were red and black and yellow and black.

Creative activities
Making ladybirds from egg boxes.
Mobile ladybirds using cheese boxes.
Pebbles painted to make ladybirds.

Mathematical follow-up
Comparison between light and heavy pebbles.
Comparison between weight of egg boxes and pebbles.
Sinking and floating—egg box and pebble.
Different sized ladybirds—grouping into families—mother, father, baby. How many in each group?
How many spots on each ladybird? Shape.

Vocabulary

more than	lighter than	bigger than	less than
heavier than	smaller than	same as	round
smooth	flat	many	few

Conversations
Elizabeth (3.0), comparing the sizes of the pebbled ladybirds.

Elizabeth: These ladybirds are small and little. These are big, big, big. The little ones are small and shiny like glass. The little ones have got little spots, the big ones have got big spots. The big ones go round and round. (She then tries to spin a small flat pebble around.)
This one won't go round and round because it's too flat.

(She then compares the sound of the egg box ladybird and the pebble ladybird.)
This one [egg box] sound like horses but this one sounds like the football when they clap. (Two pebbles banged together.)

Elaine (4.4):   I can make a round with these ladybirds. (She puts them into a circle with one in the centre.)

Teacher: Why is the ladybird in the middle?

Elaine: That's the smallest one and that's the baby. (She groups the ladybirds according to size.)
I've got four babies, five mothers and five fathers. I'm going to put the babies with the mothers.
(She proceeds to do a one-to-one correspondence, but then realises that there are more "mothers" than "babies".)
There's one baby missing.

Teacher: Let's count the mothers and babies again.

Elaine: There's not one missing. I haven't got enough babies and there are too many mothers.

Nathan (4.4):   I'm having a big fat one.

Ruth (4.5):   You're having all of them. I've got the big one. I've got four. How many have you got?

Nathan: I've got nine. I've got more than you.

Ruth: You've got more than me 'cause I've only got four. Nicola has only got one. Sara hasn't got any. I can pick all of mine up, but they're very very heavy. I've dropped one on the floor. I've only got three now.

Nathan: I've got big ladybirds and little ones.

Ruth: I've just got big ones.
(To Nicola.) You can have these two big ones. You've got three now. I've only two. I want all of them. I haven't got enough to play with. I don't like two—I like a lot.

Claire (4.6):   Let's play ring-a-ring-a-rosies with them.

Anthony (4.8):   We'll have to put them into a circle all around.

Claire: We must turn the ladybirds over when they fall down 'cause they've got to be flat on the floor. What else can we do with the ladybirds?

Anthony: Let's count them.

Claire: No, I'm going to line them up like soldiers.

Anthony: That's a very long line like a snake.

The next two examples show some mathematics which can arise from two well-known stories.

Example 2
Discussion after listening to "Three Billy Goats Gruff".

Simon (5.4):   The middle billy goat is smaller than his big brother but bigger than his little brother.

Ivan (5.3):   Yes, that's why he is called middle Billy Goat Gruff.

Example 3
Discussion after listening to "Little Red Riding Hood".

Teacher: Why did the wolf get to the cottage first?

David (4.9):   Because the little girl was picking flowers.

Josephine (4.11):   No, the wolf took a short-cut because it is quicker.

Ian (4.10):   The wolf's a better runner because he has big feet.

Ross (4.10):   It's because he has more feet than us.